The Essential Guide

to the curses,
swear words,
obscenities, insults,
profanities and
sex slang of
contemporary English

This book cannot be bought in a bookshop.
It is only available from
www.vulgarenglish.com

Buy your own copy today!!!

Vulgar English & Sex Slang

Published by Long Island Guides, 65 Elm Grove,
Brighton, East Sussex, BN2 3ET, United Kingdom

ISBN No: 0-9545960-0-5

Designed and illustrated by Simon Smith Associates, Brighton, England

Printed and bound by Antony Rowe Ltd, Chippenham, Wiltshire

10 9 8 7 6 5 4 3 2 1

Vulgar English
& *Sex Slang*

An English Language resource for the real world

Jonathan Chamberlain

A Long Island Guide

Long Island Press

Use them at your own peril!
You are warned!

"Profanity is the last refuge of the inarticulate prick."

Phil Spector, music producer

Contents

Jonathan Chamberlain has been an English language teacher for many years and is now a full-time English Language textbook writer, having authored over 30 course books.

He has also written **Chinese Gods**, an introduction to Chinese Folk religion, and **Fighting Cancer – A Survival Guide** – a critical look at orthodox cancer treatments and the alternative options. This book is supported by a website at *www.fightingcancer.com.*

Acknowledgements

A number of people have helped me with their encouragement, advice and suggestions. First among these is my son, Patrick, aged 12, who was always making suggestions for words to include. 'Have you got tosser, dad?' 'What about minger?' I don't know where he learnt these words (Well, OK, I do – the school playground) and he was equally surprised that I also knew these words: 'How do you know all these words, Dad?' he once asked.

Yes, my source for many of the words and phrases in this book is my own knowledge of the language I grew up with. However, I have also depended on a number of books. The most essential of these was **Cassell's Dictionary of Slang** by Jonathon Green (Cassell 1998). I also referred to the following books: **The F-word** by Jesse Sheidlower (Faber & Faber 1999 – first published by Random House 1995); **The Slang of Sin** by Tom Dalzell (Merriam Webster 1998); **The Big Book of Bodily Functions, The Big Book of Being Rude** and **The Big Book of Filth** by Jonathon Green (Cassell 2000); **Roger's Profanosaurus** by Anonymous (Pan Macmillan 2002) and finally the **Bloomsbury Dictionary of Euphemisms** by John Ayto (Bloomsbury 2000) and the same author's **Dictionary of Word Origins** (Arcade 1990).

It is interesting that these books have all appeared for the first time very recently.

Other individuals have helped me but they have preferred not to have their names published. I too have considered whether it would be wiser to publish under a pseudonym – John Bull, perhaps! However this is a serious book and I am happy to take personal responsibility for whatever merits or defects it may have.

Foreword

'You say funky. He says cool. She says fcuk'

No, that isn't a misprint. This is from an advertisement for
the French Connection UK chain of shops. The same company
produces a sweet alcoholic drink – Fcuk Spirit – aimed
presumably at the young woman drinker. What is she
supposed to ask for when she's ordering her drink: "Can I
have a fcuk, please?". You see the problem? How is she
supposed to pronounce this word?

The fact that this company feels able to promote itself in this
way is a sign of the new ambivalence towards vulgar
language. On the one hand it remains vulgar. On the other
hand it is becoming almost acceptable.

For language learners the situation creates difficulties. You
don't want to cause offence or use inappropriate language –
but equally you do want to understand what people are
saying. You want to understand what actors are saying in
films. And besides, let's face it, you also want to be cool.

But what is the language teacher to do about this new state of
affairs? Students want to learn these words but teachers find
it embarrassing to teach them. Unfortunately, vulgarity won't
go away if we ignore it. It is here to stay, whether we like it or
not. That is why this book on Vulgar English and Sex Slang is
needed.

Again, to make the point afresh, very recently in Britain, a
senior civil servant has been quoted in the quality press as
saying: "You're fucked. I'm fucked. We're all fucked." Both the
fact that such an eminent man should use this language and
that it should be reported in all the newspapers, including
The Times, demonstrates how mainstream the use of vulgar
language has become – though of course it was reported
largely because it was considered to be slightly shocking!

Not so long ago, President Clinton found himself in deep trouble because he encouraged a young woman to perform oral sex on him. I had the experience, at around the same time, where a teacher exploded in anger because a student had asked him what 'blowjob' meant. He didn't feel this was a suitable word for a 19-year-old girl to know about. And my student dictionary – probably the best student dictionary around – would not be of any help to that girl as it does not include the word.

Clearly there is a problem when we deprive students of some of the vocabulary they need to describe the major events of the times; words that are part of the standard vocabulary of contemporary women's magazines such as Cosmopolitan, which would certainly hope to attract 19-year-old female readers.

But vulgar language is not just about learning a dozen or so bad words. It is a complex linguistic area – and also a playful one. But it is an embarrassing one for the teacher to have to teach. Generally speaking teachers would prefer to avoid having to teach it – but students the world over like to learn the vulgarities of the language they are learning.

And, indeed, vulgar language has become so mainstream that it has become essential that they do learn it if they are to use the language properly. It is simply not safe to deprive students of information about an important slice of the language that they will come across in the street or on the internet.

This was brought home to us all when a 16-year-old Japanese student was killed in the United States a few years ago because he didn't know that 'freeze!' meant 'stop and stand still!' and was likely to be spoken by a man with a gun in his hand. It is, quite simply, much safer for students to know the current colloquial slang of the language they are learning – in this case English – and a lot of that slang is vulgar.

9

That is why this book is necessary. Students can read it and learn the words in the privacy of their own rooms.

Thirty years ago, a book on the subject of Vulgar English – a book that tried to teach all the bad words – would have been unacceptable. Today, I believe, it should not be considered merely acceptable but necessary. Vulgar English has invaded standard mainstream English just as sex has invaded popular culture. It should now no longer be considered acceptable *not* to teach this vulgar language.

This book is not about the way people should speak, or the way it would be nice if people did speak. It is about the way many people – most of us, actually – really do speak.

How is it that vulgar language has become so popular?

Thirty years ago, we taught people a version of English that was considered proper and appropriate to polite social settings. Slang and vulgar use was to a large extent swept under the carpet. When did this change? It didn't happen all at once. Certainly, the process started long ago.

Perhaps we can point to the writers James Joyce and D.H. Lawrence who, in the early decades of the last century, shocked British, Irish and American society because they wanted to use the word 'fuck' in their books. Later, in the sixties, the Nixon tapes were released to the public domain. U.S. President Nixon had got into the habit of taping every meeting and every conversation. Perhaps these would have rotted away in obscurity if it had not been for the Watergate scandal.

Nixon had, it seemed, been party to a conspiracy to cover up the theft of documents from the Democratic Party's offices in the Watergate Building. The tapes were examined for evidence and the transcripts revealed that President Nixon was virtually unable to utter even a simple sentence without using vulgar language. Of course these words were much too vulgar to appear in print so wherever there was a vulgar word or phrase in the transcript of the conversations, they were replaced with the phrase 'expletive deleted'. Vulgarity had seeped into the very heart of American government, the Oval Room of the White House itself.

It wasn't until 1970, that 'fuck' was uttered in a movie (now it is hard to find a movie that doesn't have the word). The two films that broke the fuck-barrier simultaneously were Mash and Myra Breckenridge – but Kenneth Tynan, a British theatre critic, had already uttered the word on British television as early as 1966. The rest, as they say, is history.

Current live television programmes – such as the Jerry Springer Show – show people spouting countless vulgarities and almost every Hollywood movie is jam packed with obscenities – and nobody even blinks an eyelid.

These are times when a film aimed at the teeny-bopper market can be called 'The Spy Who Shagged Me'. I know because my son, only 9 at the time, insisted on dragging me to see this film – and then he proceeded to explain every joke! We cannot go back to a supposedly more innocent past. Our children won't let us!

Here is a typical and wholly unexceptional piece of dialogue from an everyday action film that would, apart from the language, be considered acceptable viewing for most kids: Money Train, starring Wesley Snipes and Woody Harrelson.

Wesley: *You're fucked up man.*
Woody: *You're calling me a fuck up?*
Wesley: *I didn't say that, man. I said you're fucked up.*
Woody: *You think I'm a fuck up?*
Wesley: *You're not listening to me. I said you're fucked up.*

This is not brilliant dialogue but it is fairly standard. Movies, of course, now do everything they can to demonstrate their 'street-cred' – they want to be cool and knowing. And, as movies impact on their audiences – so too does the use of vulgar language become more acceptable year by year.

Of course a book such as this will always be slightly out of touch. English slang has a way of sucking in new words and phrases from many sources – and there are certain English language communities that enjoy generating new words: teenagers, gays, blacks to name a few. They are highly creative. Many words come and go – victims of their moment. Some are briefly fashionable, others are more enduring. This book cannot hope to have them all. In any case, a vulgar word that is current among US gays for example may not be easily understood without explanation among the average blue collar worker in Britain. In this book I have tried to steer a course so that the majority of the words and phrases will be widely recognised among the mainstream native-English speaking community.

Also, there are many other, non-vulgar, slang words or phrases that seem to attach themselves naturally to the area of the vulgar, words generally relating to sex, but which are not really, in themselves, at all vulgar. I have included many such words and phrases as it seemed better to do so than to omit them.

And finally, a warning: vulgar language is a taboo language. When we break taboos we are likely to shock people. Many of the words in this book have the power to shock if spoken in the wrong way or the wrong time to the wrong person. You are strongly advised to learn the words first of all for recognition. You should use the words only when you are confident that you are in a group or context where it is acceptable to do so.

Jonathan Chamberlain
Brighton

Preamble

There are many ways of referring to vulgar language – we can call it bad, dirty, crude, or obscene.

It is easy to imagine that the reason the words are 'bad' is that they refer to bad things. But this is not true. For every bad word there is generally speaking a standard or nice way to refer to the same thing. Also, of course there are bad words that refer to things that are not in themselves bad at all.

The chart on the next page gives some examples contrasting a number of vulgar words with other ways of referring to the same things – 'standard/formal' words and 'nice/familiar' words. Standard or formal words are those that a doctor or scientist might use without embarrassment, words that generally come from Latin or Greek origins. Nice words, on the other hand, are those words we might use socially in a way that would allow us to avoid the cold formality of proper words while at the same time avoiding the crudeness of the vulgar terms.

Words meaning 'vulgar language'

Profanity (adjective: profane)

Blasphemy (adjective: blasphemous)

Obscenity (adjective: obscene)

Strong language, foul language, racy language, colourful language, filthy language, dirty words, cursing, swearing, unrepeatable language.

Standard-Nice-Vulgar: An Overview

The chart below shows us a simple cross section of the way
proper words differ from nice words, both differing again from
vulgar words.

Standard	Nice	Vulgar
man	guy, bloke	prick, bastard, fucker etc
woman	girl, lady	bitch, cunt, slut etc
penis	manhood	cock, prick etc
vagina	pussy	cunt
breasts	bust	tits
sexual intercourse	make love, have sex	fuck, shag, bonk, bang etc
oral sex	give head, go down on	give a blowjob, skullfuck
semen, sperm	come (or 'cum')	jizm, spunk, jizz
to have an orgasm	to come, to climax	to shoot (one's) wad,
faeces (n)	poo, doo-doo	shit
defecate	to have a poo, do a poo	to shit
urine	wee-wee, pee	piss
urinate	have a wee/pee	
	have a leak	to piss
testicles	family jewels	balls, bollocks
buttocks,	bum, buns, butt, bottom	ass, arse
rectum, anus	bottom, bum	ass, arse, asshole, arsehole

Overview of this book

Chapter 1: *Taking the Lord's Name in Vain*
This chapter looks at the vulgar use of words that are associated with religion.

Chapter 2: *Parts of the body*
In this section we look at the vulgar ways of describing the parts of the body and some of the idiomatic uses of these words.

Chapter 3: *Sex*
Here we look at the words and phrases – and some of the associated slang expressions – that refer to sexual activities.

Chapter 4: *The F-word*
The range of idioms that use the word 'fuck' is very large. They require a chapter of their own.

Chapter 5: *Insults and Angry Words*
Here we look at the vulgar words used to insult people and express anger.

Chapter 6: *Language of the Lavatory*
In this section you will find the idioms associated with the words 'shit' and 'piss' – and other related words and phrases.

Chapter 7: *Sex Slang*
This is a miscellaneous collection of slang words – arranged alphabetically that refer in some way to sex.

TAKING THE LORD'S NAME IN VAIN

Nowadays, when we talk about cursing or swearing, we mean using vulgar or obscene language - but the original meanings of these words is very different. Cursing is literally to express the wish that some evil event should fall on someone that the speaker of the curses finds hateful.

> MAY YOU ROT IN HELL!

> A PLAGUE ON YOU!

> I HOPE HE DIES A SLOW AND PAINFUL DEATH!

Swearing, on the other hand, originally meant to use the name of God or Jesus as a guarantee that the speaker was honest, or true in some way.

> MAY GOD STRIKE ME DEAD IF I DON'T DEFEAT THE ENEMY!

> I SWEAR THAT I AM TELLING THE TRUTH

But nowadays the words 'cursing' and 'swearing' mean the same thing: the use of bad and vulgar language.

In this section we will look at the words and phrases that have a religious basis. These are usually not considered as bad as the other words that you will find in other chapters of this book. But for many people they are still ugly as they are blasphemous or profane – they 'take the Lord's name in vain' – that is, they use the name of God or Jesus in a non-religious and disrespectful way. However, religion has lost much of its hold on our lives and consequently these words have lost a lot of their force. Nowadays they are considered among the weakest of swear words and are not likely to cause terrible embarrassment or upset to anyone overhearing them. They are usually used to express mild anger or annoyance.

Here then are the most common everyday phrases that use religious words.

GOD

Key words

God!	*My God!*
Gawd!	*Oh God!*
Oh my God!	*God almighty*
Good God!	*Honest to God*
As God is my witness	*By God*
For God's sake	*God help us*
God knows	*I wish to God*
In God's name	*I swear to God*
Thank God	*God willing*
God forbid	*God-awful*
Put the fear of God into...	

God!

We say this word when we feel awed by something.

To make it even stronger we often say '**My God!**'

MY GOD, THIS BAG'S HEAVY

MY GOD, SHE'S SEXY

But God! can also be used to express a kind of agony. In this case it is spoken in a slow, drawn out way - for this reason it is sometimes written **gawd** in American stories.

Oh God!

When we put the sound 'oh' in front of God, the meaning changes. It is used commonly when we suddenly understand there has been a mistake.

This expression is not very strong in force and is not considered rude in any way - except, perhaps, if you are talking to someone who is very Christian.

Or to express worry or concern.

> DID YOU HEAR? THE 6 O'CLOCK TRAIN HAS CRASHED...

> OH GOD! I HOPE JOHN WASN'T ON IT

> I HEARD MARY HAS HAD TO GO TO HOSPITAL...

> OH GOD! I HOPE IT'S NOT SERIOUS

Oh my God!

We use this phrase to express many different types of emotion. It expresses very strong emotion.

OH MY GOD! I DON'T BELIEVE IT! I'VE WON THE LOTTERY!

OH MY GOD, I FEEL AWFUL

OH MY GOD! I WONDER HOW MUCH HE WEIGHS

God almighty!

This phrase expresses great surprise, often a good surprise.

GOD ALMIGHTY! I HAVEN'T SEEN YOU FOR AGES

GOD ALMIGHTY! WHAT A WONDERFUL SURPRISE

But it can also be used to express bad feelings or a kind of negative amazement.

GOD ALMIGHTY! I'VE GOT A TERRIBLE HEADACHE

GOD ALMIGHTY! HOW DID ANYONE SURVIVE THAT CAR CRASH?

Good God!
An expression of surprise or shock.

> GOOD GOD! IS IT 5 O'CLOCK
> ALREADY? I HAVE TO GO NOW

Honest to God!
An expression signalling that the speaker is about to criticise something.

> HONEST TO GOD! PEOPLE SHOULDN'T
> DO THINGS LIKE THAT IN PUBLIC!

As God is my witness
We use this rather formal phrase when we are insisting on the truth of something.

> AS GOD IS MY WITNESS, I HAD
> NOTHING TO DO WITH THE KILLING

> AS GOD IS MY WITNESS, I NEVER
> ASKED HIM FOR MONEY

By God
We use this phrase when we are angry and we are threatening action.

> BY GOD! I'LL SHOW HIM I CAN DO THE
> JOB AS WELL AS ANYONE CAN

> BY GOD! HE'LL REGRET THIS

For God's sake...!
This is an expression of impatience or exasperation.

> FOR GOD'S SAKE, STOP COMPLAINING!

FOR GOD'S SAKE, WHY DIDN'T YOU TELL ME YOU NEEDED SOME MONEY?

FOR GOD'S SAKE, HURRY UP!

God help us!

This is an expression of despair. When everything is bad and there's no way of improving a situation then this is what we say:

JANE REFUSES TO DO ANY REVISION FOR THE EXAM...

GOD HELP US! DOES SHE WANT TO FAIL?

I HAVEN'T GOT ANY MONEY AND I DON'T GET PAID FOR ANOTHER WEEK...

GOD HELP US! DON'T YOU PLAN YOUR FINANCES?

God knows

This means: 'I don't know'.

WHAT TIME IS HE COMING BACK?...

GOD KNOWS!

HOW MUCH MONEY HAS HE GOT?...

GOD KNOWS!

I wish to God

A strong way of saying 'I wish'.

In God's name

This phrase expresses incredulity, a mixture of shock and incomprehension.

I swear to God

A phrase used to add strong emphasis to a statement.

Thank God

We use this to express relief that something good happened or that something bad didn't happen.

MY DAD WAS IN A CAR ACCIDENT BUT HE WASN'T HURT...

THANK GOD FOR THAT!...

YES, THANK GOD

THEY STOLE MY MONEY BUT, THANK GOD, THEY DIDN'T TAKE MY CREDIT CARD

IT LOOKS LIKE IT!... IT SMELLS LIKE IT!... IT TASTES LIKE IT! ...THANK GOD I DIDN'T STEP IN IT!

God willing

If God wishes something to happen it will happen.

THIS TIME TOMORROW WE'LL BE LYING ON A BEACH IN ITALY, GOD WILLING

> YOU SHOULD GET YOUR PROMOTION SOON...

> YES, GOD WILLING

God forbid

This phrase expresses the idea that God should be opposed to some event or state of affairs.

> I HOPE JOHN DOESN'T THINK I TOOK HIS MONEY...

> YES, GOD FORBID!

> GOD FORBID THAT I SHOULD HARM MY BROTHER

God-awful

Extremely bad.

> THE FILM WAS GOD-AWFUL

> THERE WAS A GOD-AWFUL TRAFFIC JAM

Put the fear of God into someone

To frighten someone.

> IF HE GETS IN MY WAY, I'LL PUT THE FEAR OF GOD INTO HIM

> MY TEACHER IN SCHOOL PUT THE FEAR OF GOD INTO ME

GOODNESS

This is the euphemism – nicer way of saying something – for God.

Key words

My goodness!	*Goodness gracious me!*
For goodness sake	*Thank goodness*

My Goodness! Goodness gracious me!

These are expressions of surprise. 'Goodness gracious me' is slightly archaic and is associated particularly with an Indian/Pakistani style of speaking.

> MY GOODNESS! YOU HAVE LOST A LOT OF WEIGHT!

> GOODNESS GRACIOUS ME! I NEARLY DIDN'T RECOGNISE YOU

For goodness sake!

This is the polite, nice way of saying 'For God's sake'.

> FOR GOODNESS SAKE, HURRY UP! WE'RE LATE!

Thank goodness

Means the same as Thank God.

> THANK GOODNESS YOU HAD AN UMBRELLA

LORD

One way of addressing God is to call him 'Lord'.

Key words

Oh Lord!	*Lordy!*	*Lordy me!*

Oh Lord!

It is quite common to hear people use the phrase 'Oh Lord!' when they are lamenting something.

OH LORD! I WISH I DIDN'T HAVE TO GO TO SCHOOL!

OH LORD! I'M LATE!

Lordy! Lordy me!

Some people say that 'Lordy me!' is short for 'Lord help me'. These two phrases express mild to moderate surprise.

LORDY! I DIDN'T EXPECT TO SEE YOU HERE!

LORDY ME! WHAT A SURPRISE!

JESUS CHRIST

Not only do we regularly, and very casually, blaspheme against God, we also take in vain the name of the son of God.

Key words and phrases

Jesus!	*Christ!*
JesusChrist!	*Jesus H Christ!*
Jesus fucking Christ!	*Oh sweet Jesus!*
Jesus wept!	*Jesus freak*
Jeez! / Gee!	*For Christ's sake!*
Jeepers!	*Gee whiz!*

Jesus! Christ! Jesus Christ!

As an exclamation, these words are used in exactly the same way as 'God!' They express the same range of meanings: surprise, shock, sudden anger, amazement, or extreme feeling: When we say them, we tend to stress these words strongly eg: Jee-zus.

JESUS CHRIST! THAT CAR NEARLY RAN ME OVER

CHRIST! YOUR ROOM IS A COMPLETE MESS

JESUS, I'M TIRED

Americans sometimes, in a jokey way, give Jesus a middle initial (Americans like to state their middle initials – and one US president who didn't have a middle name even invented a middle initial: Harry S Truman). That's how we get: 'Jesus H. Christ' – the H doesn't stand for anything.

JESUS H CHRIST! I REFUSE TO LISTEN TO ANY MORE OF YOUR NONSENSE!

29

Sometimes people want to give it more emphasis, like this: 'Jesus fucking Christ'.

> **JESUS FUCKING CHRIST, WHAT HAVE YOU BEEN DOING TO YOURSELF?**

> **JESUS FUCKING CHRIST, WHY ARE YOU BEING SO RUDE?**

Oh sweet Jesus!

Sometimes we want to express a very strong positive emotion. In this case we can say: 'Oh Sweet Jesus!'

> **OH SWEET JESUS! THAT FEELS GOOD**

Jesus wept!

This phrase is used to express despair at being a witness to extreme stupidity.

> **JOHN TOLD THE BOSS HOW HE SHOULD BE DOING HIS JOB...**

> **JESUS WEPT!**

Jesus freak

A slightly contemptuous way of referring to a fervent Christian.

> **DID YOU HEAR! JOHN HAS FOUND RELIGION. NOW HE'S A REAL JESUS FREAK**

> **I WAS STOPPED BY TWO JESUS FREAKS BUT I TOLD THEM TO BUZZ OFF**

Jeez! Gee! Jeepers! Gee whiz!

All of these words are euphemisms for Jesus and are exclamations. The exact feeling of the exclamation will depend on context and the way it is pronounced. *Jeez!* And *Gee whiz!* tend to be complaining, *Gee!* Suggests positive feelings, *Jeepers!* Suggests surprise.

> **JEEZ! WHY DO I HAVE TO GO TO SCHOOL?**

> **GEE! WHAT A NICE SURPRISE!**

For Christ's sake...!

This has the same meaning as For God's sake, but may have a little more force. In American novels it is often written like this: 'for Chrissakes,...!'

> **FOR CHRIST'S SAKE, STOP WORRYING**

> **FOR CHRISSAKES, DON'T TELL HIM I TOLD YOU**

DAMN

This is one of the most common and weakest of swear words. It doesn't carry much force. The literal meaning of damn is that God will turn his anger on you and you will be forced to live in hell ('eternal damnation') forever. The verb is 'to damn someone', the noun is 'damnation'. Note that the final 'n' is not pronounced so the word sounds like 'dam' (but the 'n' is pronounced in the word 'damnation').

Key words and phrases

Damn	Dammit!
Damned	As near as damn it
Be damned if	Don't give a damn
Do one's damnedest	No damn good
Not worth a damn	One damn thing after another
Goddamn	

Damn! Damn it! Dammit!!

'Damn!' is used to express annoyance in general, especially a sudden annoyance.

> DAMN! DAMN! DAMN! WHY DID I DO IT? IT WAS SUCH A STUPID THING TO DO!

> OH DAMN! I'M GOING TO BE LATE FOR THE MEETING

> DAMN IT (DAMMIT)! I DON'T HAVE ENOUGH MONEY

Damn (someone)

This phrase is used to express annoyance about another person.

> DAMN JOHN! HE SHOULDN'T HAVE GOT IN MY WAY

> DAMN YOU! DON'T PRETEND TO BE MY FRIEND. DAMN YOU TO HELL!

Damn (+ adjective/adverb)

This is a rude and stronger way of saying 'very' or 'really'.

YOU KNOW DAMN WELL WHAT I MEAN

HE WAS A DAMN GOOD FRIEND

I DIDN'T HIT THE TARGET BUT I WAS DAMN NEAR

IT'S DAMN COLD

IT'S DAMN HOT HERE, ISN'T IT?

Damn (+ noun)

Damn is an intensifier of nouns also. It is another way of saying 'big' or 'great' in negative sentences.

WHAT A DAMN SHAME HE COULDN'T COME TO THE PARTY TODAY

SHE WAS A DAMN FOOL

Damned

Often, when used to give emphasis to an adjective, 'damn' becomes 'damned'

> I'M DAMNED SURE HE TRIED
> TO CHEAT ME

> HE'S DAMNED ANNOYED AND
> I DON'T BLAME HIM

As near as damn it

This is a phrase that means 'very close to'.

> IT TOOK US THREE MONTHS, AS NEAR
> AS DAMN IT, TO FINISH THE JOB

> THE BILL COMES TO $100,
> AS NEAR AS DAMN IT

Be damned if...

This phrase means 'certainly not'. 'I'm damned if I'm going to help him' means: I certainly will not help him.

> I'M DAMNED IF I'M GOING TO APOLOGISE.
> HE SHOULD APOLOGISE TO ME

> I'M DAMNED IF I'M GOING TO
> BE NICE TO HIM

The same phrase can also express a certain surprise that you can't do something that you perhaps thought you could do. For example: 'I'm damned if I know the answer' means 'I don't know the answer and that surprises me.'

> *I'M DAMNED IF I CAN REMEMBER HIS NAME*

> *I'M DAMNED IF I CAN MAKE THIS RADIO WORK*

Don't give a damn

This phrase means 'don't care at all' about something.

> *I DON'T GIVE A DAMN WHO HE IS*

> *JOHN DOESN'T GIVE A DAMN ABOUT HIS JOB*

Do one's damnedest

To do one's best to achieve something. Often there is a suggestion that the effort was unsuccessful.

> *HE DID HIS DAMNEDEST TO GET ME THE JOB BUT THAT WASN'T GOOD ENOUGH UNFORTUNATELY*

> *I DID MY DAMNEDEST TO CATCH HER EYE BUT SHE REFUSED TO LOOK AT ME*

No damn good

This is a strong way of saying something is no good.

> *MY CAR IS NO DAMN GOOD ANY MORE. I'LL HAVE TO GET ANOTHER ONE*

> *I'M NO DAMN GOOD AT TENNIS*

Not worth a damn

Worthless.

> THIS COIN ISN'T WORTH A DAMN

> HIS GUARANTEE ISN'T WORTH A DAMN

One damn thing after another

Emphasising a succession of bad events.

> I HAD A TERRIBLE DAY TODAY. IT WAS JUST ONE DAMN THING AFTER ANOTHER

Goddamn

This combination of God and damn, making a new word, is more typically American than British. It is stronger in force than 'damn' on its own so it expresses more anger and a greater sense of violence. It is most commonly used as a simple utterance 'goddamn it!' or as an intensifier.

> GODDAMN IT! I TOLD YOU NOT TO BE LATE. YOU SHOULD HAVE BEEN HERE TEN MINUTES AGO

> WHO DO YOU THINK YOU ARE? THE GODDAMN POPE?

> WHERE'S THE GODDAMN CAR?

Euphemisms for 'damn'.
Key words

Darn   Dash

Darn

Sometime, long ago, somewhere in America, the word 'damn' must have seemed too vulgar, or too irreligious, or just too rude to use in polite society.

But what do you say when you feel the need to express a certain irritation? Well, in America they invented a word that sounded vaguely similar to damn but which was sufficiently different for it to be used in polite society. That word was 'darn'.

It is so weak in force that it can be used with children present without any suggestion of embarrassment. In fact it sounds folksy – that is, it sounds nicely traditional and unthreatening and even polite (because it shows sensitivity in avoiding that nasty word 'damn').

We call words like this 'euphemisms' – polite (or nice) ways of referring to something that is not nice. Here are some examples:

OH DARN IT! I'VE LEFT MY WATCH AT HOME

THAT DARNED CAR NEARLY CRASHED INTO US! WE DARN NEAR HAD AN ACCIDENT

Dash

This is the British euphemism for 'damn'. It is very old fashioned and typical of elderly or conservative middle-aged, middle-class men. It is almost always used as an expression of anger: 'Dash it all!' or as an adjective 'dashed'. (Meaning: very, extremely.)

> DASH IT ALL! PEOPLE SHOULDN'T HAVE TO SLEEP ON THE STREETS!

> I WAS THERE WITH MY WIFE ON ONE SIDE AND MY GIRLFRIEND ON THE OTHER. IT WAS DASHED AWKWARD

BLOODY

Key words and phrases

Bloody	Bloody nerve
Bloody good thing	Bloody well
Bloody-minded	Blooming
Blithering	Bleeding

Bloody

This is almost always used as an intensifier and it is a little stronger than 'damn' so it expresses a little more anger.

> THAT BLOODY MAN REALLY ANNOYS ME

> WHAT A BLOODY NUISANCE

> I'VE BEEN A BLOODY FOOL

To have a bloody nerve:

This is a common utterance that you say to someone who has betrayed your trust in some way or shown disrespect.

> YOU'VE GOT A BLOODY NERVE ASKING
> ME FOR MONEY. YOU STILL OWE ME $100

Bloody (+ adjective)

It can also be used simply to add force to an adjective (but not necessarily suggesting anger). Here, like 'damn', it is used instead of 'very'. Note that it can be used to express positive as well as negative messages.

> SHE CAN BE REALLY BLOODY
> ANNOYING SOMETIMES

> WHAT A BLOODY STUPID IDEA

> THAT'S A BLOODY GOOD BOOK.
> YOU SHOULD READ IT

Bloody great big

This combination of words means 'very, very big'.

> IT WAS A BLOODY GREAT BIG
> SPIDER. IT REALLY SCARED ME

> IT'S A BLOODY GREAT BIG BUILDING.
> YOU CAN'T MISS IT

It's a bloody good thing that...

A strong way of saying 'It's good that...'

> ITS A BLOODY GOOD THING YOU
> BOUGHT THIS BOOK! NOW YOU KNOW
> HOW TO SWEAR IN ENGLISH

Bloody well

This phrase is used to insist that something has happened or will happen.

> I'M NOT GOING TO MAKE MY BED...

> OH YES, YOU BLOODY WELL WILL

> I'VE NEVER LIED TO YOU...

> OH YES YOU BLOODY WELL HAVE

> YOU'RE NOT GOING TO TELL JOHN, ARE YOU?...

> OH YES, I BLOODY WELL AM

Bloody (+ verb)

As an emphasiser, 'bloody' or 'bloody well' can also appear before verbs – especially verbs suggesting anger. A polite version would be to replace these words with 'really'.

> HE BLOODY ANNOYS ME

> HE BLOODY WELL IRRITATES ME

To be bloody minded
This means to be stubborn or unreasonably persistent.

> JOHN CAN BE REALLY BLOODY
> MINDED SOMETIMES!

> DON'T BE SO BLOODY MINDED!

Euphemisms for 'bloody'.
Key words

Blooming	Blithering	Bleeding	Ruddy

Blooming
'Blooming' is only used by very polite people and can be used in the following phrases:

> YOU'VE GOT A BLOOMING NERVE!

> YOU ARE BLOOMING WELL GOING TO
> DO SOME WORK!

> HE HAD A BLOOMING GREAT SCAR
> ACROSS HIS FACE

Blithering
Only really used with the word 'idiot'.

> YOU BLITHERING IDIOT!!!!

Bleeding

This is specifically working class English.

> WHAT'S THE BLEEDING PROBLEM?

> BLEEDING HELL!

HELL

This is one of the classic bad words of the old days. Hell is where the devil lives – and in the days when God and the devil were – or seemed to be – part of everyday life, the thought of Hell would have carried great force. Who would want to spend time in this hot and sulphurous place? Now, of course, Hell seems rather remote to most atheistic Europeans and consequently the word doesn't carry as much force as it used to. In the old days, Hell was spelled with a capital H. But as a swear word we normally spell it with a small 'h' – unless of course it starts a sentence.

Key words

Hell!	*Oh hell!*
Bloody/fucking hell!	*Go to hell*
Hellish	*It was hell*
What the hell	*Well, hell*
Like hell	*All hell broke loose*
For the sheer hell of it	*Give someone hell*
Hell for leather	*Hope to hell*
Hell of a	*Hell hole*
Hell's bells	*Raise merry hell*
The (thing) from hell	*There will be hell to pay*
To hell with it	*Sure as hell*
Heck	

Oh hell!

This is what you say when you're angry about something. The force of the meaning depends on how much emphasis and force you use in saying the word. If you say the word quickly and loudly it has strong force. If it is said slowly and softly, the emotion it expresses is tiredness or acceptance.

Bloody hell

And we can – and often do - make hell stronger by adding 'bloody'.

Fucking hell

This means the same but is even stronger in feeling.

> **OH FUCKING HELL! WHY DID I DO THAT?**

> **FUCKING HELL! THAT WAS LUCKY!**

Notice in the examples above that we use the 'oh' sound when what we are going to say has a negative meaning. Without the 'Oh' sound, the message may be positive or negative.

Go to hell

If you're angry with someone and you want to reject everything they are saying and you don't want to have anything to do with that person then you say: 'Go to hell'.

> **THERE'S A MAN OUTSIDE WHO WANTS TO SELL YOU SOME INSURANCE...**

> **TELL HIM TO GO TO HELL**

> **I WANT YOU TO DO ME A FAVOUR...**

> **GO TO HELL! I'M NOT DOING YOU ANY FAVOURS**

Hellish, hellishly

These are the adjective and adverb forms.

> **IT WAS A HELLISH EXPERIENCE**

> **IT WAS HELLISHLY DIFFICULT TO GET TO SEE THE BOSS**

It was hell!

This expression is a way of saying that something was a very unpleasant and uncomfortable experience.

THE JOURNEY WAS HELL!

MY MARRIAGE WAS HELL!

What the hell...?

This is a very common use of 'hell'. It is added to questions – the questions that start with 'who', 'what', 'how', 'where', 'when' – to make them sound angrier.

WHAT THE HELL DO YOU WANT?

WHO THE HELL TOLD YOU THAT?

HOW THE HELL DID YOU GET THE MONEY TO BUY THAT SPORTS CAR?

WHERE THE HELL DID I PUT MY ADDRESS BOOK?

WHEN THE HELL ARE YOU GOING TO GET A JOB?

WHY THE HELL SHOULD I LEND YOU ANY MORE MONEY? YOU NEVER PAY ME BACK

Well, hell...!

We use this phrase when replying to someone who has made a silly suggestion or expressed a stupid opinion or said something that makes us a little annoyed.

> I NEED SOME MONEY...

> WELL, HELL! WHY DON'T YOU ASK YOUR DAD? HE'S STINKING RICH

> MARY REFUSES TO TALK TO ME...

> WELL, HELL! THAT'S NOT MY FAULT

...hell!

Hell can be used to show total disagreement with something.

> MARY GAVE YOU A LOT OF SUPPORT...

> SHE DID HELL! SHE SUPPORTED EVERYONE EXCEPT ME

> YOU'RE WINNING THE GAME...

> I AM HELL! I'M GOING TO LOSE EVERYTHING SOON

> YOU CAN SPEAK GERMAN...

> I CAN HELL! I CAN SAY PERHAPS THREE WORDS AND THAT'S ALL

Like hell!
This has the same meaning of expressing disagreement or even refusal.

> IT WAS A GREAT FOOTBALL MATCH...

> LIKE HELL IT WAS! IT WAS THE WORST MATCH I'VE SEEN IN A LONG TIME

> IT'S YOUR TURN TO WASH THE DISHES...

> LIKE HELL IT IS! I WASHED THEM AT LUNCHTIME

(To do something)...like hell
Usually this phrase adds emphasis to an act requiring speed.

> I RAN LIKE HELL DOWN THE HILL

> HE DROVE LIKE HELL ALL THE WAY TO THE BEACH

The hell...!
This is another phrase that is used to emphasise a negative response – usually a refusal to do something or a denial.

> JOHN WON THE FIGHT...

> THE HELL HE DID! JAMES WAS ON TOP OF HIM THE WHOLE FIGHT

> TOM'S THE BEST SWIMMER...

> THE HELL HE IS! HE ONLY WON ONE RACE. I'VE WON THREE

What the hell!

This phrase can be said at the beginning, or in the middle of a statement, and it means, 'Oh alright, I may not want to (do this thing) but I'll do it and accept the consequences.'

> LET'S GET MARRIED...

> OH OK, WHAT THE HELL, WHY NOT?

> COME ON! LET'S GO TO DANCING CLASSES...

> OK, WHAT THE HELL, IF THAT'S WHAT YOU REALLY WANT TO DO

All hell broke loose

Chaos or pandemonium – a sudden outbreak of shouting and screaming.

> THE WORLD CHAMPION WAS KNOCKED OUT IN THE FIRST ROUND AND ALL HELL BROKE LOOSE!

> THE MALE STRIPPERS TOOK OFF THEIR CLOTHES AND ALL HELL BROKE LOOSE!

For the (sheer) hell of it

For the fun of it.

> WE RAN NAKED ACROSS THE FOOTBALL FIELD. WHY? JUST FOR THE SHEER HELL OF IT!

Give (someone) hell

This means to shout at someone for doing something wrong.

> HE GAVE ME HELL FOR MAKING
> THE MISTAKE

> I'M GOING TO GIVE HIM HELL!

Hell for leather

To go very fast.

> WE DROVE HELL FOR LEATHER
> TO THE HOSPITAL

> HE RAN HELL FOR LEATHER
> DOWN THE STREET WITH THE GANG
> OF BOYS CHASING HIM

Hope to hell

This is a way of adding force to the verb 'hope'.

> I HOPE TO HELL I PASS THE EXAM

> I HOPE TO HELL NOTHING BAD HAPPENS

A hell of a...

This phrase, surprisingly, has a very positive meaning, suggesting that something is very good. It can also be written as one word, helluva.

> IT WAS A HELL OF A PARTY. I CAN'T REMEMBER HOW I GOT HOME

> IT WAS A HELL OF A FILM. ABSOLUTELY AMAZING

> WE HAD A HELL OF A GOOD TIME

> YOU'RE A HELL OF A DANCER. YOU'LL HAVE TO TEACH ME SOME STEPS

Note that the plural form drops the first 'a'.

> WE WERE HELL OF A GOOD FRIENDS

Hellhole

A very unpleasant place.

> THE BROCHURE SAID IT WAS A GOOD HOTEL BUT IT WAS AN ABSOLUTE HELLHOLE

Hell's bells!

Just a phrase expressing surprise or annoyance – not very vulgar.

> HELL'S BELLS! I FORGOT TO GET HER TELEPHONE NUMBER

Raise merry hell

This phrase can mean a variety of things:
a) to cause a lot of trouble,
b) to scold someone severely and
c) to celebrate in a rowdy way.

> THE TWO YOUNG CHILDREN RAISED MERRY HELL ALL DAY LONG

> JOHN'S MOTHER RAISED MERRY HELL WHEN SHE FOUND OUT HE HAD STOLEN SOME MONEY

> THE SUCCESSFUL STUDENTS CELEBRATED IN THE MIDDLE OF TOWN, RAISING MERRY HELL UNTIL LATE AT NIGHT

The (thing) from hell

The most terrible example of something.

> SHE WAS THE LANDLADY FROM HELL. SHE REALLY WAS AWFUL

> I HATED MY NEIGHBOUR'S DOG. IT WAS THE DOG FROM HELL

There will be hell to pay

A prediction of very bad consequences.

> THERE'LL BE HELL TO PAY IF I DON'T GO HOME TONIGHT. MY WIFE WILL KILL ME!

To hell with...

This is an exclamation of anger or dismissal.

> TO HELL WITH YOU!

> TO HELL WITH THE EXAM — LET'S GO AND HAVE A DRINK

Sure as hell

This means 'certainly'.

> HE SURE AS HELL DESERVED TO WIN FIRST PRIZE

> IF I DO ANYTHING WRONG, SURE AS HELL, SOMEONE WILL CATCH ME

Euphemism for hell.

> *Heck*

Just as darn is a euphemism for damn, so heck is a euphemism for hell. But we can't replace all of the uses of hell with heck because heck doesn't have any real meaning. So we can say:

> OH HECK! I'VE LEFT MY WATCH AT HOME

> WHAT THE HECK HAVE YOU DONE TO YOUR HAIR?

> WELL HECK! I FEEL I DESERVE AN APOLOGY

> WHAT THE HECK, I'M GOING TO QUIT MY JOB!

But we can't say:

> IT WAS A HECKISH MEETING

> ALL HECK BROKE LOOSE!

> GO TO HECK!

Or maybe I shouldn't say we can't say these because American newspapers are capable of anything. I have just seen a headline in one that said: 'All heck broke loose!'. This just sounds silly.

HOLY...!

There are a number of exclamations that start with 'Holy! The vulgar forms are common in both UK and USA but the nice versions tend to be used only in the USA.

Nice   *Holy cow!, Holy mackerel!, Holy Moses!, Holy moly!*
Vulgar   *Holy shit!, Holy fuck!*

> HOLY SHIT! WHAT HAPPENED TO YOU?

> HOLY FUCK! THAT CAR WAS GOING FAST

Irish Swear Words

It is sometimes said that the Irish don't really speak English but rather their language is Gaelic in translation. This certainly seems true of some of their Irishisms below which are typical of Ireland and nowhere else.

Bejazus

Swear word which is used generally in the same way as 'Jesus!'. But can also replace words like 'shit' when used to add emphasis.

> **BEJAZUS! I NEARLY GOT KNOCKED DOWN BY THAT CAR!**

> **I KICKED THE BEJAZUS OUT OF HIM**

Other typically Irish exclamations of surprise or of despair:

> **BEGORRAH! WHAT A SURPRISE!**

> **JESUS, MARY AND JOSEPH! DID YOU SEE THAT!!!?**

> **MARY, MOTHER OF GOD! WHAT IS THE WORLD COMING TO?**

Other Irish vulgarities

Bollix

An Irish spelling of 'bollocks' (see Chapter 2) but used to refer insultingly to people.

> YOU'RE A BOLLIX

Eejit

Idiot.

> DON'T BE AN EEJIT!

Gobshite

A general insult.

> HE'S A FUCKING GOBSHITE. THAT'S WHAT HE IS

Shite!

The Irish version of 'Shit' (see Chapter 6).

> HE'S A SHITE!

> WHAT A SHITE!

Baloney

Nonsense.

> SHITE. THIS IS HEAVY

Old fashioned Exclamations

These words are specifically British and are used as expressions of surprise or mild annoyance.

Crikey! Blimey! Cor Blimey! Strewth! Cripes!

These words are specifically American and again indicate surprise.

Jiminy Cricket! Holy Moly! Gee whiz! Sheesh!

Other old fashioned swear words

Blast

An utterance of anger. Less forceful than damn.

OH BLAST! I'VE SPILLED COFFEE ON MY SHIRT

OH BLAST! I CAN'T FIND MY BRIEFCASE

Blasted

This is used as an intensifier to give emphasis:

THAT BLASTED MEETING WENT ON AND ON

THE BLASTED TAXI DRIVER REFUSED TO STOP AND GIVE US A LIFT

Blighter

Very old fashioned English word meaning bad man – a polite way of saying bastard.

Curses

The word 'curse' itself is used as a swear word.

Curses!

An exclamation – especially used in the written form in old fashioned polite stories.

The curse

A slang term for a woman's monthly menstrual period.

SHE'S NOT FEELING VERY WELL. SHE'S GOT THE CURSE

Cuss

An American dialect version of curse. It is used in the following ways.

To cuss: to swear
A cuss: a bad person
Don't give a cuss: don't care

IT'S BAD MANNERS TO CUSS IN A CHURCH

I DON'T GIVE A CUSS WHAT YOU THINK

THE STUPID CUSS TRIED TO HIT ME

Chapter 2: *Parts of the body*

PARTS OF THE BODY

There are a lot of words that refer to parts of the body – specifically to the sexual differences between men and women. Some of these words are also used in vulgar expressions with other meanings. In this chapter we will contrast the 'proper' words for each part of the body – the words that a scientist or doctor would use – with the 'nice' words that someone might use in any situation without causing offence and the 'vulgar' words which would be considered not acceptable in polite society. We will look first at the male body, then later at the female body.

ADAM & EVE

The Male Body

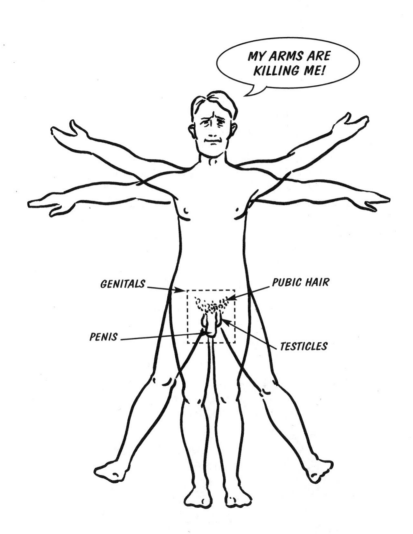

Genitals

Proper word:
Genitals (male).

Nice version:
Private parts, privates, bits and pieces, bits.

Slightly vulgar:
Naughty bits, wobbly bits, crown jewels, family jewels, vitals, packet, package, cods, meat and two veg*, tackle, wedding tackle, lunchbox, fruitbowl, dangly bits.

---

*Note: this is a joke: 'meat and two veg' is a standard description of a standard English meal – 'veg' is an abbreviation for vegetables.

Penis

> **Proper word:**
> Penis.
>
> ---
>
> **Nice version:**
> Manhood, male organ, male member.
>
> ---
>
> **Slightly vulgar:**
> Willy (often used with children), Peter, Percy, John Thomas, instrument, weapon, doodle, thing, thingy, whatsit, doodah.
>
> ---
>
> **More vulgar:**
> Cock, prick, dick, pole, pecker, nob (also: knob), tool, dong, ding-dong, wick, dipstick, the one-eyed monster, whang, whanger, fuck muscle, love muscle, pego, todger, fuck rod, schlong, joy stick, chopper, skinhead, bacon bazooka, pork sword, spam javelin, mutton musket, one-eyed trouser snake, shaft, third leg, middle leg, love truncheon, purple headed warrior, weiner.

THE DOCTOR LOOKED AT MY PENIS

MY SON CAUGHT HIS WILLY IN HIS TROUSER ZIP

HE FORGOT TO CLOSE HIS ZIP, AND I SAW HIS JOHN THOMAS

Vulgar Expressions

COCK

This is the most common vulgar word for penis. It is also the name of a male chicken. Almost certainly there is a connection. The sexual prowess of a rooster is well known.

Key words and phrases

A cock up	To cock (something) up
Cocky	Cocksucker

A cock up

This means that something was done badly and the result is bad in some way.

THERE WAS A COCK UP SOMEWHERE AND HALF THE STUDENTS DIDN'T TAKE THE EXAM

I DON'T WANT ANY MORE COCK UPS

IT WAS A COCK UP FROM START TO FINISH

To cock something up / cock up something

This is the verb form and has the same meaning as the noun above.

THEY COCKED UP THE BOOKING SO WE COULDN'T ALL STAY IN THE SAME HOTEL

EVERYTHING MUST GO SMOOTHLY. DON'T COCK ANYTHING UP

Cocky

Arrogant.

HE'S A COCKY BASTARD

DON'T BE SO COCKY!

Cocksucker

This literally refers to someone who will have oral sex with a man. But it is also used as a term of contempt.

STAY AWAY FROM HIM! HE'S A COCKSUCKER

DICK

Key words and phrases

Dick	*Dickhead*
Dickbrain	*Dickface*
Dick breath	*To dick someone*
Dick around	*Dick (someone) around*
To dick (something) out	*Dickless*
Dick shit	*Dick thing*
Big swinging dick	

'Dick' is much more commonly used in America than Britain, where 'cock' is more common.

Dick

This is an old American slang word for police detective – a dickless Tracy is a woman police officer. This is a complex joke: Dick Tracy was a cartoon detective; Tracey is a common girl's name.

Dick / dickhead / dickbrain / dickface

General terms of abuse which refer to someone as a contemptible person. Stupid person, fool.

> HEY DICKHEAD!

> GET AWAY FROM ME, DICKBRAIN

> GO TO HELL, DICKFACE

Dick breath

Someone contemptible who has bad breath.

> I WISH I DIDN'T HAVE TO
> TALK TO DICK BREATH

To dick someone

To cheat or deceive someone. Dick is also the standard nickname for people called Richard. This explains the following graffiti that appeared towards the end of President Richard Nixon's career during the Watergate investigations.

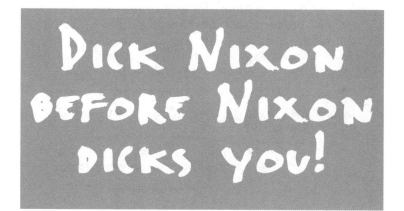

To dick around

To fool around. To refuse to be serious.

> STOP DICKING AROUND. WE
> HAVE WORK TO DO

> DON'T DICK AROUND WITH ME.
> IF YOU DO, YOU'LL BE SORRY!

To dick someone around

To cause someone problems, to be unhelpful.

> STOP DICKING ME AROUND,
> WILL YOU?

> HE HAS DICKED ME AROUND FOR
> THE LAST TIME. I'M GOING TO GET
> HIM FOR THIS!

To dick (something) out

To continue to do something that is difficult until you get to the end of it – to persevere. The non-vulgar way of saying this is: to stick (something) out. The fact that dick rhymes with stick probably explains how this phrase came into existence.

> IT WAS A TOUGH JOB BUT
> I DICKED IT OUT

> I KNOW IT'S A DIFFICULT SITUATION
> BUT PLEASE TRY TO STICK IT OUT

Dickless

A general term of abuse suggesting cowardice or the absence of male virtues.

> HE'S SUCH A DICKLESS IDIOT!

> DON'T BE SO DICKLESS! JUST ASK HER FOR A DATE!

Dick shit

This means 'nothing at all' - often used with a negative verb.

> I'VE GOT DICK SHIT TO DO

> YOU DON'T KNOW DICK SHIT ABOUT ANYTHING!

Dick thing

This phrase refers to subjects that are of interest to men but of no interest to women. Often the word 'thing' is pronounced 'thang' to make it sound like the accent of the southern states of America.

> THIS DOESN'T INTEREST YOU, MARY? I GUESS IT MUST BE A DICK THING

Big Swinging Dick

This phrase refers to the boss, the person on top of the pecking order, the person everyone else must give respect to.

> WHO'S THE BIG SWINGING DICK AROUND HERE?

KNOB

With knobs on

This is used as an angry retort to someone and has the meaning: the same to you and more so.

YOU'RE A FOOL...

AND THE SAME TO YOU WITH KNOBS ON!

PECKER

Key words and phrases

> To have someone's pecker in your pocket
>
> To keep one's pecker up

To have someone's pecker in one's pocket

U.S. President, Lyndon B Johnson, made this phrase famous when he said of another politician: 'I've got his pecker in my pocket'. He meant that he had control of the politician's vote. See 'to have someone by the balls' (page 74).

To keep one's pecker up

To be positive or brave.

I'VE BEEN FEELING A BIT LOW SINCE SUSAN LEFT ME...

COME ON! DON'T BE MISERABLE! YOU'VE GOT TO KEEP YOUR PECKER UP

PRICK

This is commonly used as an insult.

> JOHN IS A PRICK. DON'T TRUST HIM

WICK

'To get on one's wick' means to make someone angry.

> HE REALLY GETS ON MY WICK SOMETIMES

> JULIA REALLY GETS ON TOM'S WICK

Testicles

Proper word:
Testicles.

Nice version:
The gonads, the crown jewels, the family jewels.

Vulgar version:
Balls, bollocks (also spelt 'ballocks'), marbles, stones, rocks, nuts, goolies, pillocks, plums, apricots, cobblers, cods, conkers, nads, pills, pods.

> STOP FIDDLING WITH YOUR MARBLES! GET YOUR HANDS OUT OF YOUR POCKET!

Vulgar expressions

BALLS

Key words and phrases

Balls!	*Oh balls!*
Balls to that!	*Ball breaker*
Ball buster	*Ball crusher*
A balls up	*To ball (someone)*
To balls (something) up	*To break (one's) balls*
To break (someone else's) balls	*To have balls*
To have someone by the balls	*To have brass balls*
To have one's balls to the walls	
To kick someone in the balls	
To make a balls of something	
To work (one's) balls off	
Cold enough to freeze the balls off a brass monkey	

Balls!
A way of expressing strong disagreement.

> ENGLAND WILL WIN THE
> NEXT WORLD CUP...

> BALLS! THEY HAVEN'T GOT
> A CHANCE

> I'M THE GREATEST!...

> WHAT A LOAD OF BALLS!

Oh balls!
This is what you might say when you have made a mistake or you are unhappy about something.

> OH BALLS! I'VE SENT THE LETTER
> TO THE WRONG ADDRESS

> OH BALLS! THE COFFEE
> MACHINE IS BUST

Balls to that!
A phrase of contemptuous dismissal.

> JOHN WANTS YOU TO
> APOLOGISE TO HIM...

> BALLS TO THAT!

A ball breaker
A hard boring job.

> HOW'S THE NEW JOB GOING?...

> IT'S A BALL BREAKER!

A *ball buster*

Someone who makes us work hard.

> MY NEW BOSS IS A REAL
> BALL BUSTER

A *ball crusher*

A woman who likes to dominate men.

> MARGARET ALWAYS DOMINATES HER
> BOYFRIENDS. SHE'S A REAL BALL CRUSHER

A *balls up*

A mess (the same as 'cock up').

> NO-ONE PAID ANY ATTENTION TO THE PROBLEM
> SO NATURALLY THERE WAS A BIG BALLS UP

> THE MEETING WAS A BIG BALLS UP.
> NO-ONE WAS LISTENING TO WHAT THE
> OTHER SIDE WAS SAYING

To ball someone

To have sex with someone. It can also be used in an intransitive way.

> I WOULDN'T MIND BALLING HER

> WE BALLED

To balls something up

To make a mess of something. Notice that the word balls is always plural.

> **JOHN BALLSED UP THE ARRANGEMENTS AND WE COULDN'T GET A HOTEL ROOM**

> **IT WASN'T OUR FAULT. JAMES BALLSED IT UP, NOT US**

To break one's balls

To work very hard at something.

> **I BROKE MY BALLS TO GET THE JOB FINISHED ON TIME**

To break someone else's balls

To damage them in some way that hurts. To destroy someone.

> **IF HE GETS IN MY WAY, I'LL BREAK HIS BALLS**

To have balls

To be brave.

> **HE'S GOT A LOT OF BALLS TO DO WHAT HE DID**

> **I DIDN'T HAVE THE BALLS TO STAND UP TO HIM**

Ballsy

Brave.

> **SHE'S A BALLSY GIRL**

To have/get someone by the balls

To have someone in your complete control.

> JOHN WON'T DO ANYTHING TO STOP ME.
> I'VE GOT HIM BY THE BALLS

> I'VE GOT TO DO WHAT HE SAYS.
> HE'S GOT ME BY THE BALLS

To have one's balls to the walls

To be undergoing a very stressful time.

> HOW'S THE NEW JOB...?

> IT'S TERRIBLE. I'VE REALLY GOT MY
> BALLS TO THE WALLS. I'M WORKING TEN
> TO TWELVE HOURS A DAY

To have brass balls/balls of brass

To be cheeky – to do things that no-one else would dare to do.

> JOHN'S GOT BALLS OF BRASS.
> NOTHING BOTHERS HIM!

> YOU'VE GOT TO HAVE BRASS BALLS
> TO SUCCEED IN THIS BUSINESS

To kick someone in the balls

This can be meant literally or metaphorically. If meant metaphorically it would mean that someone has caused another person pain where it hurts most.

> I HEAR JOHN'S GONE OFF WITH
> YOUR GIRLFRIEND...

> YEAH. HE'S REALLY KICKED
> ME IN THE BALLS

To make a balls of something
To make a mess of something.

> I DIDN'T GET THE JOB BECAUSE I MADE A BALLS OF THE INTERVIEW

To work one's balls off
To work very hard.

> I'M WORKING MY BALLS OFF AT THE MOMENT BUT THINGS SHOULD CALM DOWN NEXT MONTH

Cold enough to freeze the balls off a brass monkey
This phrase just means what it says: it is very cold.

> IT WAS FREEZING LAST NIGHT...

> YES. IT WAS COLD ENOUGH TO FREEZE THE BALLS OFF A BRASS MONKEY

BOLLOCKS

This is another word for balls, and sometimes it is spelt 'ballocks'.

Key words and phrases

Bollocks!	**Oh Bollocks!**
A load of bollocks	**To bollock (someone)**
To give (someone) a bollocking	
To make a bollocks of (something)	
Big bollocks	

Bollocks!
A way of expressing complete disagreement.

JOHN'S REALLY NICE, DON'T YOU THINK?...

BOLLOCKS. HE'S A COMPLETE PRICK IF YOU ASK ME

Oh bollocks!
A common swear word expressing irritation or mild anger.

OH BOLLOCKS! THIS COMPUTER KEEPS CRASHING

A load of bollocks
'Nonsense!'

IN MY OPINION MIKE TYSON WAS THE GREATEST BOXER EVER...

WHAT A LOAD OF BOLLOCKS!...

I AGREE. THAT'S THE BIGGEST LOAD OF BOLLOCKS I HAVE EVER HEARD!

To bollock somebody / To give someone a bollocking
To shout at somebody for making a mistake. To give someone a reprimand.

I BOLLOCKED HIM FOR ARRIVING LATE FOR THE MEETING

I GAVE HIM A GOOD BOLLOCKING FOR BEING RUDE TO THE CUSTOMER

To make a bollocks of (something)

The means to make a mess of something, to do something badly.

I MADE A BOLLOCKS OF THE
SPEECH. IT WAS AWFUL!

The big bollocks

This can either mean a 'fool' or 'an important man'.

WHO IS THE BIG BOLLOCKS
AROUND HERE?

NUTS

The testicles appear to have been named after every kind of small round object: rocks, marble – and nuts (such as peanuts, brazil nuts etc). Nut (singular) also means the head (as in such phrases as 'use your nut!', 'he's a nutcase' and so on). When nuts is used in the plural form it generally refers to the testicles.

Key words and phrases

Nuts!   Be nuts about (something)   To bust one's nuts

Nuts!

This can express disappointment

YOU'VE GOT TO WORK LATE THIS EVENING...

OH NUTS!

Nuts! / Nuts to that!

Nonsense! Rubbish!

I'M GOING TO WIN THE RACE...

NUTS!

WE'RE ALL GOING TO HAVE TO ACCEPT A PAY CUT...

NUTS TO THAT!

Be nuts about (someone/something)

To like someone or something to the point of obsession. This is not at all vulgar.

JOHN IS NUTS ABOUT JAZZ. HE'S GOT OVER 1,000 CDS

I'M NUTS ABOUT YOU!

To bust one's nuts

This is modern American slang for having an orgasm (male).

> **I BUST MY NUTS TWICE LAST NIGHT!**

Erection

Proper word:
Erection.

Nice version:
(Proud) manhood, get hard.

Vulgar versions:
Hard on, horn on, root on, boner, prong, pronger, stand, cock stand, stiffie, stand to attention.

> **I GET A HARD ON JUST THINKING ABOUT HER**

> **I'VE GOT TO DO SOMETHING ABOUT THIS BONER**

> **HE'S GOT A REAL HORN ON**

The Female Body

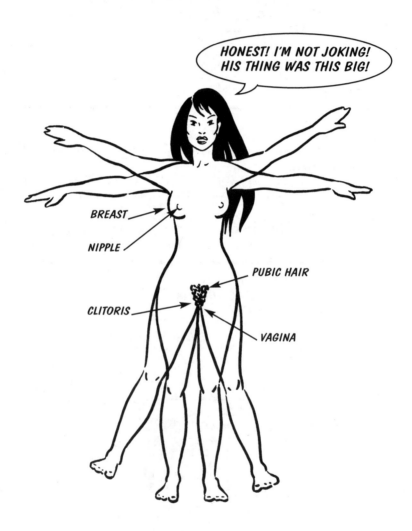

Breasts

Proper word:
Breast(s).

Nice version:
Breast(s), bosom, bust.

Slightly vulgar:
Tits, boobs, jubblies, natural assets.

Vulgar:
Hooters, bristols, bubbies, knockers, lungs, gazungas, gazonkas, bazongas, bazonkas, juggs, wham danglers, norks, norkers, norkies, wombles, funbags, mammaries, udders, melons, watermelons, coconuts, apples, grapefruit, headlamps.

Vulgar English & Sex Slang

Vulgar Expressions

TIT

This word is only slightly vulgar and it is quite common for women themselves to refer to their 'tits'.

Key words and phrases

A tit	*To make a tit of oneself*
To get on (one's) tits	*To keep (one's) tits on*
Tough titty!	

Tit

A fool.

> *JOHN CAN BE A RIGHT TIT SOMETIMES*

Tit

This is an old English word that came from German. Originally it meant nipple and the related word 'teat' still has this meaning.

> *I WAS A COMPLETE TIT. I'M SORRY*

To make a tit of oneself

To make a fool of oneself.

> *I MADE A COMPLETE TIT OF MYSELF. IT WAS VERY EMBARRASSING!*

To get on one's tits

To make one angry.

> *JOHN ANNOYS ME. HE REALLY GETS ON MY TITS*

To keep one's tits on!
'Don't be angry!' – usually said by a man to a woman.

> *I'M REALLY ANGRY WITH YOU!...*

> *JUST KEEP YOUR TITS ON!*

Tough titty!
An expression showing lack of sympathy.

> *JOHN WON'T LEND ME ANY MONEY.*
> *I HAVEN'T GOT A CENT ON ME...*

> *TOUGH TITTY! YOU SHOULD HAVE THOUGHT OF*
> *THAT BEFORE YOU STARTED YELLING AT HIM*

Buxom

Description of woman with large breasts (approving)

> *SHE'S A BUXOM GIRL*

Other ways of referring to a woman who is buxom:

Nice:
Voluptuous, curvaceous, shapely, has a good figure.

Slightly vulgar:
Busty.

Vulgar:
Stacked, has great big hooters, built like a brick shithouse.

Vagina

Proper word:
Vagina, female genitals.

Nice version:
Treasure, holy of holies, pudendum.

Slightly vulgar:
Pussy, cunny, honeypot, punani (US black or West Indian), purse, futz, bliff, badger.

Very vulgar:
Cunt, fanny*, twat, hole, slit, gash, cleft, quim, poon, box, snatch, fur pie, nookie, notch, minge, nun's wink, poozle, gluepot, fur burger, hairy pie.

Note: In US English 'fanny' means a woman's bottom while in UK English it refers to the vagina

Vulgar expressions

CUNT

a) An insulting way of referring to a woman.

I FANCY A PIECE OF THAT CUNT

b) An insulting word referring to a man or woman that the speaker considers contemptible.

JOHN'S A COMPLETE CUNT

WHAT A CUNT!

Cunt

The first time this word appeared in English was in about 1230 as the name of a street 'Grope Cunt Lane', presumably a narrow lane where men would fondle women. There was one in Oxford and another in London. It appears to be a word of German origin.

Her Cuntliness...

According to an article in Rolling Stone magazine, it seems that some of the younger male actors in the film Lord of the Rings found the word 'cunt' intoxicating and made a point of using it whenever they could when they were off the set. They even referred to one of the leading actresses as 'Her cuntliness'. (ref: The Queen: Her Royal Highness; The Pope: His Holiness). When asked how she reacted to this, the male actor replied: "It was an honour."

NOOKIE

This word can refer to a woman, to the vagina and also to the act of sex:

woman:

> THERE'S A NICE LOOKING PIECE OF NOOKIE

vagina:

> I GOT MY HAND ON HER NOOKIE

sex:

> I HAD SOME NOOKIE LAST NIGHT

TWAT

Twat

Fool.

> JOHN'S A COMPLETE TWAT

Twat around

To spend a lot of energy achieving very little - or wasting time.

> STOP TWATTING AROUND

MINGE

This can refer to both the vagina and to a woman.

Minge-bag

An insulting way of referring to a woman.

> SHE'S A COMPLETE MINGE BAG

Minge winker

A stripper.

> LET'S GO INTO THIS BAR AND CHECK OUT THE MINGE WINKERS

Clitoris slang

Bean	*pink*	*love button*

The View From the Back

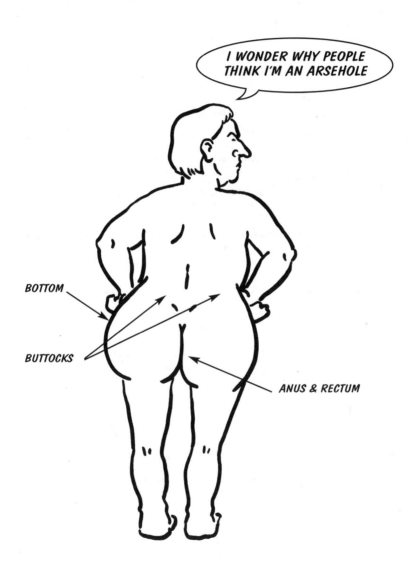

Buttocks

Proper word:
Buttocks**.

Nice versions:
The derrière*, bottom, behind, cheeks.

Slightly vulgar:
Butt, buns, rear, rear end, backside, rump, booty, botty (for children), tush (U.S. Jewish), hindquarters, posterior.

Vulgar version:
Ass, arse***, bum, batty, keister (U.S.), muffins.

---

* *This is a French word.*

** *Note that some of these words are plurals (buttocks, buns) while others tend to refer to the area as a singular item (butt, bottom) – the two halves are called 'cheeks'.*

*** *'ass' is American and 'arse' is British.*

Vulgar expressions

BUM

Key words and phrases

Bum	Bummer
A bum (something)	Bummed out
To bum (something)	To bum around
To bum (something) off (someone)	
To be given the bum's rush	Get up (one's) bum
A bum freezer	

A bum

A person who has no job, who lives on the streets, is dirty etc. By extension it can also mean a nasty person.

I FEEL SORRY FOR THAT BUM. HE JUST LOOKS SO SAD

WHAT DO YOU MEAN YOU'RE NOT GOING TO HELP ME. YOU CAN BE A REAL BUM SOMETIMES

Bummer!

A bad experience.

I LEANT HIM MY CAR AND HE CRASHED IT INTO A LAMPPOST...

WHAT A BUMMER!

THAT SUMMER I LOST MY JOB, MY HOME AND MY GIRLFRIEND. IT WAS A REAL BUMMER!

A bum (something)

Fake, invented or just no good.

> THE OLD LADA WAS A REALLY BUM CAR
> BUT THE NEW ONE IS QUITE GOOD

Bummed out

'To be bummed out' is to be really angry. More common in USA.

> WHEN I DISCOVERED THE TRUTH,
> I WAS REALLY BUMMED OUT

Three common American phrases

A bum steer:

Misinformation or bad advice.

> HE GAVE US SOME INFORMATION BUT
> IT TURNED OUT TO BE A BUM STEER

A bum rap:

False accusation or an unfair decision against someone.

> I WAS ACCUSED OF CHEATING BUT I DIDN'T
> CHEAT! HONEST! IT WAS A BUM RAP!

A bum deal:

A bad arrangement.

> I PAID FAR TOO MUCH MONEY FOR THE CAR.
> IT WAS A BUM DEAL

To bum a lift

To get a ride in a car to some place you want to go. The non vulgar way of saying this is to 'hitch a lift'.

> **HOW DID YOU GET HERE FROM LONDON?...**

> **I BUMMED A LIFT IN A TRUCK**

To bum around

To have fun doing nothing much.

> **WHEN I WAS YOUNG I JUST BUMMED AROUND ALL SUMMER LONG**

> **THE LAST I HEARD OF JOHN HE WAS BUMMING AROUND THE SOUTH OF FRANCE**

To bum something off somebody

To get something from somebody by begging.

> **I BUMMED A CIGARETTE OFF HIM**

> **COULD I BUM FIFTY PENCE OFF YOU. I'M OUT OF SMALL CHANGE**

To get (or be given) the bum's rush'

This means to be thrown out of a place or to be forced to leave very quickly.

Get up (one's) bum

To become annoyed.

A bum freezer

A short jacket that just comes down to the waist.

BUTT

Key words and phrases

Butt out	*Butthead*
Buttfuck	*Butt plug*
Butt pussy	*Butt slut*
Butt wipe	*Buttkicking*
Butt ugly	*To butt fuck*
To butt suck	*To move / shift one's butt*
To park (one's) butt	

Butt out!

Don't interfere.

HEY! WHAT'S UP? WHAT'S HAPPENING?...

JUST BUTT OUT! GO AWAY! IT'S NONE OF YOUR BUSINESS

Butthead!

Fool or idiot. It can be used as a description or as an insult.

HEY BUTTHEAD! GO FUCK YOURSELF!

JOHN WAS A REAL BUTTHEAD LAST NIGHT

Buttfuck

A disaster.

> THE MEETING WAS A COMPLETE BUTTFUCK. NOW THE SITUATION IS EVEN WORSE THAN IT WAS BEFORE

Buttkicking

Strong, powerful and aggressive. It can also be used as a verb phrase: to kick butt *(see below)*.

> THE TEAM PUT ON A REAL BUTTKICKING PERFORMANCE AND WE WON BY A BIG MARGIN

To butt-suck / to suck butt

To do everything to be nice to one's boss etc. The standard term for this is to kiss ass. A person who behaves in this way is a butt-sucker, arse-licker or ass kisser.

> THE PROBLEM WITH JOHN IS THAT HE LIKES PEOPLE WHO SUCK BUTT

To kick butt

To be strong and powerful and aggressive – and victorious.

> LET'S KICK SOME BUTT!

> I'M GOING TO KICK BUTT!

Butt ugly

Very ugly.

> GOD, SHE WAS BUTT UGLY

To move/shift (one's) butt

To move. This can mean simply to move a little bit or it can mean to hurry up.

> SHIFT YOUR BUTT! I WANT TO SIT DOWN

> MOVE YOUR BUTT! WE'RE LEAVING IN TWO MINUTES

To park (one's) butt

To sit down.

> COME AND PARK YOUR BUTT OVER HERE

Also:

To buttfuck
To have anal intercourse.

Butt plug
A rubber object placed in the anus during sex games.

Butt pussy
A homosexual term for the anus.

Butt slut
This refers to either a man or a woman who has a strong liking for anal intercourse.

Butt wipe
Toilet paper (also: arse wipe).

Rectum/anus

Proper word:
Rectum, anus.

Nice Version:
Bottom, back passage, back door, khyber*.

Vulgar version:
Ass, arse, asshole, arsehole, butthole, fudge tunnel,
tradesman's entrance, back door.

*Note: this is an example of British rhyming slang - Khyber Pass = Arse.

> THE DOCTOR PUT HIS FINGER
> RIGHT UP MY BACK PASSAGE

> MY ASSHOLE IS REALLY PAINFUL

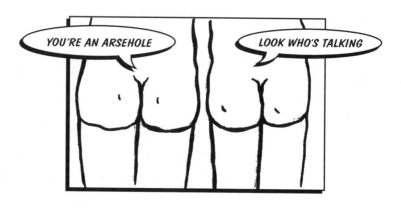

> YOU'RE AN ARSEHOLE

> LOOK WHO'S TALKING

Vulgar Expressions

ASS/ARSE

Key words and phrases

Exclamations:
Blow it out your arse!, kiss my ass!, my arse!, up your arse.

Nouns:
Arse, asshole, arse licker, piece of ass, pain in the ass.

Verb phrases:
To arse around, to be assed if, can't be assed to,
to bet one's ass, to be up to one's ass, to chew someone's ass off,
to fancy the arse off someone, to get it in the ass,
to get off one's ass, to get one's ass in gear, to kick ass,
to make an arse of oneself, to move one's ass,
to put one's ass on the line, to talk out of one's ass,
to watch (one's) ass, to work one's ass off.

Others:
Arse about tit/face/on backwards, arse over tit, arseways,
arse-holed, arsehole of the universe, bad ass, dumb ass,
half-assed, hard ass, kickass, lard ass, on one's ass,
tightass/tightassed, up (one's) own ass.

Exclamations

Blow it out your arse!

A phrase expressing contempt for what another person is
saying.

I THINK YOU SHOULD...

JUST BLOW IT OUT YOUR ARSE! I
DON'T CARE WHAT YOU THINK!

97

Kiss my ass!

A phrase of rejection and repudiation.

I'M AFRAID I'M GOING TO HAVE TO FIRE YOU...

KISS MY ASS! I'M GIVING YOU MY RESIGNATION RIGHT NOW

My arse!

An exclamation expressing disagreement.

I DID YOU A BIG FAVOUR!...

MY ARSE! IT WAS ME WHO DID YOU THE FAVOUR

Up your arse! Up yours! Stick (or shove) it up your arse!

These are vulgar, and aggressive, ways of challenging someone in a dismissive way.

EXCUSE ME, CAN YOU LET ME THROUGH PLEASE...

UP YOURS!

I THINK YOU'RE A BIT DRUNK...

STICK IT UP YOUR ARSE, MATE!

Noun Forms

Be an ass/arse. Make an ass/arse of yourself

To be stupid.

I'M SORRY, I WAS A COMPLETE ASS!

HE MADE A COMPLETE ARSE OF HIMSELF!

An asshole

An unpleasant person, or someone who acts unpleasantly.

> STOP THAT! YOU ARE BEING
> AN ASSHOLE!

> JOHN IS A COMPLETE ASSHOLE.
> DON'T HAVE ANYTHING TO DO
> WITH HIM

An ass licker

Someone who is always trying to please his boss.

> I'M NOT BEING AN ASS LICKER. I JUST
> DO THINK THE BOSS IS RIGHT

Piece of ass

An attractive girl or woman.

> WHO WAS THAT NICE PIECE OF ASS
> I SAW YOU WITH LAST NIGHT?

> LOOK AT THAT PIECE OF ASS!

Arse

This is a very old word. It comes from the very earliest Indo-European and so many European languages have a similar sounding word with a similar meaning. The American variation, 'ass', only appeared in the 1930s as a euphemism for arse.

Pain in the ass

A very annoying person or situation.

> JOHN CAN BE A REAL PAIN IN THE
> ASS SOMETIMES

> I DON'T WANT TO DO IT BUT I'VE GOT TO
> DO IT. IT'S A REAL PAIN IN THE ASS

Verb forms

To arse around

To not take something seriously, to fool around.

> WHAT DID YOU DO THIS MORNING?...

> NOTHING. WE JUST ARSED AROUND THE
> SHOPPING MALL FOR A FEW HOURS

> STOP ARSING AROUND AND START
> DOING SOME SERIOUS WORK

To be assed if

To absolutely refuse to do something. Two other phrases: 'be damned if...' and 'be fucked if...' have the same meaning but the first is less vulgar and the second is more vulgar than 'be assed if...'.

> I'M ASSED IF I'M GOING TO BE NICE
> TO HIM. I HATE HIS GUTS

Can't be assed to

Can't be bothered to (do something) – i.e. I won't do it because I'm not interested in doing it.

To bet one's ass

To bet on a sure thing.

YOU CAN BET YOUR ASS I'M GOING TO HAVE FUN TONIGHT

To be up to one's ass

The polite – and more graphic – versions of this phrase are 'to be up to one's eyes' (or 'neck' or 'here' (accompanied by a flat hand gesture above the eyes) – meaning you have too much of something.

I'M UP TO MY EYES IN WORK

HE'S UP TO HIS ASS IN DEBT

To chew someone's ass off

To give someone a severe reprimand. Also to 'chew someone's balls off'.

THE BOSS WAS REALLY FURIOUS WITH ME! HE REALLY CHEWED MY ASS OFF

HEY! DON'T GO CHEWING MY BALLS OFF! IT WASN'T MY FAULT!

To fancy the arse off someone

'To fancy someone' is to find a person sexually attractive. 'To fancy the arse off (someone)' is a stronger way of saying the same thing. Another variation is: 'to fancy the pants off someone'.

To get it in the ass

To be punished severely.

> IT WASN'T A SERIOUS CRIME BUT THE JUDGE SENT HIM TO PRISON FOR FIVE YEARS. HE REALLY GOT IT IN THE ASS

To get off one's ass

This means to stop doing nothing and start doing something.

> GET OFF YOUR ASSES AND DO SOME WORK

> FINALLY HE GOT OFF HIS ASS AND DID SOME WORK

To get one's arse in gear

To get organised.

> GET YOUR ARSE IN GEAR. WE'RE
> LEAVING RIGHT NOW

> MY SON TAKES FOREVER TO GET HIS
> ARSE IN GEAR IN THE MORNING

To get one's ass...over here / out of here etc.
to move one's ass

These phrases just mean 'move over here' or 'get out' To
move one's ass just means 'get a move on' or 'hurry up'.

> MOVE YOUR ASS. IT'S TIME TO GO

> MOVE YOUR ASS OVER HERE. I
> WANT TO TALK TO YOU

> GET YOUR ASS OUT OF HERE.
> I WANT TO BE ALONE

To kick ass

Someone who kicks ass is prepared to shout, hit, push and
whatever else it takes to make things happen the way he
wants them to happen.

> I'M YOUR NEW BOSS AND I AM
> HERE TO WARN YOU: I AM GOING
> TO KICK ASS

> I KICKED SOME ASS AND I
> GOT RESULTS. PRODUCTIVITY
> ROSE BY 20%

To kick ass has another meaning: to win conclusively.

> *THEY THOUGHT THEY WERE GOING TO WIN BUT WE KICKED ASS. THE FINAL SCORE WAS 3 – 0 TO US*

To put one's ass on the line

To take personal responsibility for something or to take a personal risk.

> *HE REALLY PUT HIS ASS ON THE LINE FOR ME SO I OWE HIM A BIG FAVOUR*

To talk out of one's ass

To talk nonsense.

> *DON'T LISTEN TO HIM. HE'S JUST TALKING OUT OF HIS ASS!*

To watch (one's) ass

A piece of advice to be careful – i.e. to watch out for what might be happening behind one's back. The polite version is 'to watch one's back'.

> *OFFICE POLITICS IS REALLY BAD. I'M HAVING TO WATCH MY ASS ALL THE TIME*

To work one's ass off!

To work hard. Other variations are: to work one's butt off.

> *I WORKED MY ASS OFF FOR TWENTY YEARS AND NOW I'M REAPING THE PROFITS*

> *I WORKED MY BUTT OFF FOR HIM AND HE NEVER ONCE SHOWED HIS APPRECIATION*

Other forms

Arse about tit

To have something back to front. Another phrase with the same meaning is 'arse about face'.

> HE'S GOT THE STORY COMPLETELY ARSE ABOUT TIT

> YOU'VE GOT YOUR PULLOVER ON ARSE ABOUT FACE

Arse on backwards

A rude way of saying confused or wrong.

> I THINK JOHN IS A NICE GUY...

> YOU'VE GOT YOUR ARSE ON BACKWARDS. JOHN IS A COMPLETE CUNT

Arse over tit

A description of someone falling over.

> I TRIPPED AND FELL ARSE OVER TIT DOWN THE SIDE OF THE HILL

Arseholed

A crude way of saying 'drunk'.

> I FEEL TERRIBLE THIS MORNING. I GOT COMPLETELY ARSEHOLED LAST NIGHT

Arsehole of the universe
A very unpleasant place.

> WHAT DO YOU THINK OF BIRMINGHAM?...

> IT'S THE ARSEHOLE OF THE UNIVERSE

Arseways
To move backwards.

> WE ALL HAD TO MOVE ARSEWAYS
> OUT OF THE ROOM

Badass
An adjective used to describe a person with a mean, aggressive attitude.

> I WAS STOPPED BY A REAL BADASS
> POLICEMAN

> AVOID HIM. HE'S GOT A BAD ASS
> ATTITUDE ABOUT EVERYTHING

Dumbass
Stupid.

> THAT'S A REALLY DUMBASS QUESTION

Half-assed
Careless or incompetent.

> HE DID THE WORK IN A HALF-ASSED WAY
> SO I'VE GOT TO DO IT ALL OVER AGAIN

Hard ass

An unpleasantly aggressive person.

> *DON'T BE SUCH A HARD ASS*

Kickass

In America, kickass can be used as an adjective to mean really good, much better than any competition.

> *IT'S A KICKASS DANCE CLUB*

> *I LOVE TAI CHI. IT'S A REALLY KICKASS SPORT*

Lard ass

A person with a fat bottom.

> *THE MAN SITTING NEXT TO ME ON THE PLANE WAS A REAL LARD ASS. IT WAS VERY UNCOMFORTABLE*

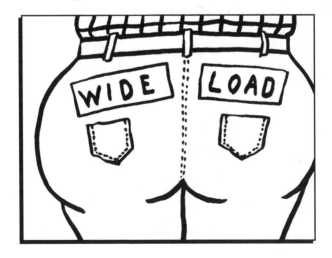

On (one's) ass

To annoy with continual attention, to pester.

> **MY BOSS IS ON MY ASS ALL DAY. IT'S DRIVING ME CRAZY!**

Tightass

A mean person. (also: tightwad). The adjective is tightassed.

> **JOHN WON'T HELP YOU. HE'S A REAL TIGHTASS**

> **HE'S A TIGHTASSED BASTARD**

Up (one's) own ass

Arrogant, self-satisfied, egotistical.

> **I REALLY DON'T LIKE HER. SHE'S SO UP HER OWN ASS**

Miscellaneous expressions

Get your finger out!

This is a phrase you say when you want people to start doing something faster. The idea is that their finger is stuck in their rectum.

> **HURRY UP! GET YOUR FINGER OUT!**

Shafted

being cheated or harmed in some – not very specific – way.
Occasionally also used in the active form 'to shaft someone'.
The original idea behind this phrase is that someone has put
a wooden handle aggressively up another person's rectum.

I THOUGHT I KNEW WHAT I WAS DOING BUT I GOT SHAFTED

HE REALLY SHAFTED YOU

IF YOU'RE NOT CAREFUL, HE'LL SHAFT YOU

Wedgie

'To have a wedgie' is to be in the uncomfortable situation
where one's underpants have risen up between the buttocks.
'To give someone a wedgie' is a practical joke in which
someone pulls another's underpants up between their
buttocks.

I HAD A WEDGIE. IT WAS VERY UNCOMFORTABLE

I GAVE JOHN A WEDGIE. HE WAS FURIOUS!

Moon

to expose one's buttocks to other people for fun or as a sign
of contempt.

WE ALL TOOK OUR PANTS DOWN AND MOONED HIM – JUST FOR A LAUGH

SEX

Given the ambivalence with which we view sex – it oscillates between the poles of 'good' (love) and 'bad' (pornography) with frightening speed (contrast also the difference between the exquisite and secretive intensity of private personal experience and the often prudish jokiness of public expression) – it is no surprise that the area of sexual intercourse is replete with vulgarity.

Standard words

To have sexual intercourse.

This is the the standard, non-vulgar term to describe this activity.

But there are two other standard words that have a similar meaning but carry a negative tone of disapproval:

To copulate/copulation

This word generally applies to animals, so when it applies to humans it carries the sense that they are behaving like animals.

To fornicate/fornication

This word refers to having sex outside marriage.

Nice words

Then there are the 'nice', non-proper, but not too vulgar
ways of referring to sex:

Have sex	*Do it*
Get it on	*Make love*
Make out	*Sleep with*
Go to bed with	*Fool around*
Get physical	*Bed (someone)*
Have a bit of rumpy pumpy	

I HAVEN'T HAD SEX IN A LONG TIME

I WOULDN'T MIND DOING IT WITH HER

LAST NIGHT LINDA AND I GOT IT ON. IT WAS GREAT!

WE MADE LOVE ALL NIGHT LONG

JOHN AND SHEILA ARE BUSY. THEY'RE MAKING OUT

TOM AND ALISON ARE FINALLY SLEEPING TOGETHER

CASANOVA SLEPT WITH HUNDREDS OF WOMEN IN HIS LIFETIME

DO YOU WANT TO GO TO BED WITH ME?

LET'S FOOL AROUND

LET'S GET PHYSICAL

HE FINALLY BEDDED HER

Vulgar words
Key words and phrases

Fuck	Screw	Shag
Bonk (Boink)	Ball	Bang
Get off	Have it off	Get laid
Hump	To boff (someone)	Roger

There are a large number of vulgar ways of referring to sex. Some of these words can be used in a number of different ways:

a) As a transitive verb (i.e. a verb that has an object):
   He ___ed her / she ___ed him.

b) As an intransitive verb (i.e. a verb that has no object):
   They ___ed.

c) As a noun:
   We had a ___.

Some words and phrases can be used in all three ways while others can't, so I will give a number of examples to demonstrate the range of possible uses of each word.

Fuck

This is the most common English vulgarity (see Chapter 4 for the many idiomatic ways in which it is used in English). In the old days, this action of fucking was something that men did to women. However, these days a woman would probably say 'I fucked him' rather than the more passive form 'He fucked me'.

> THEY FUCKED ALL NIGHT LONG

> HE FUCKED HER

> I HAVEN'T HAD A FUCK IN AGES

Fuck

It is sometimes said that no other word exceeds the word 'fuck' in the richness of its use. Not only is it used in a great many phrases but its meaning very largely depends on the intonation with which it is said.

The word is not ancient 'Anglo-saxon' as some people believe – according to historian Robert Lacey 'There are absolutely no swear words or obscenities in Anglo-saxon English' – but then the only records were kept by monks! Other people have claimed that fuck derived as an acronym. The story is told of sailors who caught syphilis being removed from ships and having the letters f.u.c.k. tattooed on their hands. The letters were supposed to stand for 'For Unlawful Carnal Knowledge'. There is absolutely no truth to any part of this story.

'Fuck' entered the English language before 1400 probably from Germany - but also possibly from Scandinavia.

Screw

This is an aggressive word and has the alternative meaning of to cheat someone. It can also be used as an aggressive challenge.

I FINALLY GOT TO SCREW HER LAST NIGHT

JOHN AND MARY ARE BUSY. THEY'RE SCREWING

SUSY IS A GOOD SCREW

Screw

'Screw' has a number of other common uses:

(i) Meaning to cheat.

> JOHN SCREWED ME OUT OF MY SHARE OF THE BUSINESS

(ii) An aggressive challenge.

> SCREW YOU!

> TELL JOHN TO GET SCREWED!

Shag

> I HAD A GOOD SHAG LAST NIGHT

> JOHN IS SHAGGING JULIA THESE DAYS

> JOHN AND JULIA ARE SHAGGING

Bonk (US: Boink)

> THEY'RE BONKING

> DID YOU MANAGE TO BONK HIM?

> WE HAD A QUICK BONK

Ball

I BALLED HER

WE BALLED FOR OVER AN HOUR

Note: It is possible to say 'we had a ball' but this refers to another meaning of ball – a large formal dance party – and the phrase means to have a good time – but it could be said as a pun 'We had a ball!' combining the two senses.

Bang

I FANCY BANGING HER

THEY'RE BANGING EACH OTHER

Get off

I GOT OFF WITH HIM

Have it off

THEY'RE HAVING IT OFF

I HAD IT OFF WITH HER

Get laid

I GOT LAID LAST NIGHT

SHE'S A GOOD LAY

Hump

> I WOULDN'T MIND GIVING HER A HUMP

> JACK AND JILL SPENT ALL DAY YESTERDAY HUMPING

Roger

> HE ROGERED HER IN THE BATHROOM

> HE SAYS HE GAVE JANE A GOOD ROGERING

Other words

Naturally, there are many other words and expressions that refer to sexual intercourse – especially as seen from the male point of view. Here are some things that men might say to themselves as they look at an attractive woman. They are all very vulgar and would be considered unacceptably gross by most women.

(i) Some use verbs that express the idea of a strong physical action by the male: pump, pound, drill etc.

> I'D PUMP HER ASS ANY DAY

> I WOULDN'T MIND POUNDING HER ASS

> I'D LIKE TO GRIND HER FANNY

> I'D LIKE TO DRILL THE ASS OFF HER

(ii) Other phrases suggest simply the insertion of the penis.

I'D LIKE TO GIVE HER A POKE

I WOULDN'T MIND SHAFTING HER

I COULD NAIL HER

I COULD PLUG HER HOLE

I WOULDN'T MIND SLIPPING HER A LENGTH

I'D LIKE TO GIVE HER A GOOD ROOT

(iii) Other expressions are less easy to categorise

I'D LIKE TO GET MY END AWAY WITH HER

I WOULDN'T MIND GETTING A BIT OF LEG OVER WITH HER

I'D LIKE TO GET INTO HER PANTS

I'D LIKE TO GIVE HER THE OLD ONE-TWO

I FANCY A BIT OF RUMPY-PUMPY

(iv) Other phrases that refer to sexual intercourse

Less vulgar:
*To get jiggy with (someone), to have a roll in the hay,
to get (someone) in the sack, to do the business with (someone),
to have (someone), to make it with (someone).*

More vulgar:
*To pork, bone, dork (someone),
to give (someone) a porking, boning, dorking.*

Inviting someone to have sex

Here are some ways in which a person – male or female – might suggest that it's time to consider having sex.

LET'S GO TO MY PLACE AND FOOL AROUND

LET'S GET HORIZONTAL

LET'S DO IT

LET'S MAKE OUT

LET'S DO THE NAUGHTY

LET'S GET DOWN AND DIRTY

LET'S GET IT ON

LET'S GO TO BED

LET'S GET IT TOGETHER

LET'S DO SOMETHING NICE AND SLOW AND INTIMATE

WILL YOU SLEEP WITH ME?

Oral sex

Oral sex has its own vocabulary. The formal words for oral sex are:

Fellatio: oral sex performed on a man.

Cunnilingus: oral sex performed on a woman.

(i) Words for when a woman (or man) gives a man oral sex:

Vulgar words:

Less vulgar:
Blow job, give head.

Slightly vulgar:
Give)someone) a chewy.

Very vulgar:
Skull fuck, skull job, gob (hob) a knob, smoke a bone, woof it.

> SHE GAVE HIM A BLOW JOB

> SHE CAN GOB MY KNOB ANYTIME

> SHE KNOWS HOW TO HOB A KNOB

> SHE GIVES GOOD HEAD

> SHE SURE KNOWS HOW TO WOOF IT!

(ii) Words for when a man or woman gives oral sex to a partner of either sex:

Key words and phrases

Go down on	*Suck someone off*
Give someone a tongue bath	*To tongue someone*
To give someone a tongue job	

HE WENT DOWN ON HER

I'M GOING TO SUCK YOU OFF

I TONGUED HER

SHE GAVE ME A GOOD TONGUE JOB

I LIKE TO GIVE MY LOVER A TONGUE BATH

(iii) Words for when a man (or woman) gives oral sex to a woman:

Key words and phrases

Muff dive	*Eat pussy*
Lick someone's clit	*Eat someone out*

HE LIKES TO EAT PUSSY

I WANT TO LICK YOUR CLIT

HE ATE ME OUT

HE'S A REALLY GOOD MUFF DIVER

YOU CAN SIT ON MY FACE ANY TIME

YOU CAN DIVE INTO MY MUFF ANY TIME

Variations:

Sixty-nine

When both lovers are simultaneously giving oral sex to each other then this is a position known as sixty-nine. Sometimes we use the French 'soixante-neuf'. This can be used as a verb or a noun.

Anal sex

In formal English, this activity is known disapprovingly as 'pederasty' and the person who engages in this activity is known as a pederast.

Vulgar words for pederast – usually in a homosexual context:

Anal astronaut	*Mud packer*
Fudge packer	*Brown pipe engineer*
Fart catcher	*Arse mechanic*
Botter	*Back seat driver*

Another word that refers to aggressive anal sex is 'buggery' (the concept), 'to bugger' (verb) and 'a bugger' (the person). But this word has lost a lot of its force. It is not considered to be very vulgar any more and is used in a number of phrases that have nothing to do with anal sex (see page 134).

The action of anal sex can be described with the following vocabulary:

Key words and phrases

> ***To ream (someone's) ass***   ***To have some bum fun***

> *HE ATTEMPTED TO BUGGER ME*

> *I'M GOING TO REAM YOUR ASS*

> *LET'S HAVE SOME BUM FUN*

Solitary sex

But sometimes a man or woman doesn't have a partner to have sexual intercourse with. They have to take things into their own hands.

Masturbation

This is the proper word meaning to give oneself sexual pleasure. The nice phrase is 'playing with oneself'. In the old days it wasn't considered proper to talk about masturbation so it would be referred to as 'onanism' (after the Biblical figure, Onan, of whom it was written: 'he spilt his seed on the ground'), or 'self-abuse' or 'self-pollution' or 'the solitary vice'. There are a large number of expressions used to describe this activity. The following list is not exhaustive but it gives an idea of the variety:

When men do it

The main slang word for masturbation is 'wank'.

> **HE'S WANKING**

> **HE'S HAVING A WANK**

Other expressions refer to the use of the hand:

> **HE'S GIVING HIMSELF SOME HAND RELIEF**

> **HE'S GIVING HIMSELF A HAND JOB**

Then there are a range of phrasal verbs using the preposition 'off':

He's whacking off	*He's beating off*
He's tossing off	*He's frigging off*
He's flipping off	*He's getting his nuts off*
He's jacking off	*He's yanking off*
He's bringing himself off	*He's jerking off*

Finally, there are the phrases which express rather picturesque images:

He's pulling his plonker	*He's pumping the python*
He's playing with percy	*He's playing his flute*
He's varnishing his flagpole	*He's milking his doodle*
He's whipping off a wad	*He's spanking the monkey*
He's beating his meat	*He's choking the chicken*

When women do it

And of course women do this too, but they're not so coy about it – they don't mind calling it by the proper name – so they haven't developed such a wide range of slang expressions for this activity. However, there are some:

She's frigging herself	*She's basting the tuna*
She's beating the beaver	*She's buttering the muffin*
She's tickling her fancy	*She's flicking her clit*
She's pleasuring herself	
She's doing a bit of cunt cuddling	
She's diddling her bean	*She's tickling her pink*

*'frig/frigging' while these words are sometimes used as euphemisms for 'fuck', they also have the specific meaning of masturbating or using the hand e.g. 'She frigged him' suggests that she used her hand to give him pleasure. This usage has been current at least since early Victorian days and can be found in a lot of the pornography of that time.)

The Big O

The ultimate objective of sexual intercourse is to have an orgasm.

Key words and phrases

To come	To cum	To climax

DID YOU COME?

IT WAS GREAT. I COULDN'T STOP CUMMING!

SHE CLIMAXED SEVERAL TIMES

OH YES! YES! YESYESYES!

Semen

When a man has an orgasm, he ejaculates semen. The Bible refers to it as 'seed'. Here are some vulgar words for semen.

Key words and phrases

Jizz (gizz)	*Jizm (gism)*	*Spunk*
Cum	*Wad*	*Load*
Gunk	*Goo*	*Cream*
Splooge	*Spoo*	*Spooch*
Joy juice	*Love juice*	*Spaff*
Spadge	*Spongle*	*Spungle*
Baby gravy		

Vulgar expressions describing a man's orgasm:

HE CAME

HE BLEW HIS LOAD

HE BLOBBED OFF

HE CRACKED HIS NUTS

HE CHUCKED HIS LOAD

HE CREAMED HIMSELF

HE GOT HIS COOKIES OFF

HE GOT HIS JONES OFF

HE GOT HIS NUTS OFF

HE BUST HIS NUTS

HE GOT HIS ROCKS OFF

HE POPPED HIS CORK

HE POPPED HIS COOKIES

HE SHOT HIS WAD

HE SHOT OFF

Spunky

This is a good example of how certain words change their meaning over time and cease to be vulgar. To be spunky now means to be brave – presumably like a young male who is 'full of spunk'. But nowadays it would not seem at all strange for a very polite and well brought up woman to use this word.

Other examples of this changing of meaning over time are the words 'comely' and 'fetching'. These are now considered to be rather old fashioned words meaning attractive.

However, these words derive from two verbs that both mean to have an orgasm:

To come, to fetch (someone)

SHE'S A VERY COMELY GIRL

SHE'S VERY FETCHING

Wank and Toss

These are the most common British slang words for masturbation. Jerk and Jerk off are the most frequently used Americanisms. These words also have other meanings.

Key words and phrases

Wanker	*Tosser*	*Jerk/Jerk off*
Big wank	*Wank mag*	*Wanky*
Don't give a toss	*Not worth a toss*	

A *wanker*

A stupid person who is no use to anyone. (Also: Jerk, Jerk off, tosser).

DON'T BE A WANKER

HENRY'S A WANKER

HE'S A JERK

HE'S A JERK OFF

HE'S A TOSSER!

A *big wank*

This is used to describe anything that gives pleasure to the person who did the action – and no real pleasure to other people.

I THOUGHT THE FILM WAS JUST A BIG WANK FROM START TO FINISH

Wanky

This means inferior quality, second rate.

I DON'T LIKE THE DÉCOR AT THE NEW RESTAURANT. IT'S REALLY WANKY

Don't give a toss

This phrase means 'don't care'.

> I DON'T GIVE A TOSS WHO WON THE ELECTION.
> ALL POLITICIANS ARE THE SAME TO ME

Ways of saying 'I don't care!'

I don't give a fuck	*I don't give a shit*
I don't give a toss	*I don't give a fig*
I don't give a damn	*I don't give a monkey's*
I don't give a tinker's cuss	

> I DON'T GIVE A FUCK WHAT
> HE THINKS OF ME

> I DON'T GIVE TOSS IF I NEVER
> SEE HIM AGAIN

> I DON'T GIVE A DAMN
> WHO HE IS

Not worth a toss

This means something is worthless or not worth getting excited or angry over.

> A POUND COIN USED TO BUY LOTS OF
> THINGS. NOW IT'S NOT WORTH A TOSS

> I SHOULD GET ANGRY WITH JOHN
> BUT IT'S NOT WORTH A TOSS

133

Bugger

Literally this word refers to sex involving penetration of the rectum. The word can be a noun ('a bugger' is a person who does this to someone else) or a verb ('to bugger' someone). The abstract noun is 'buggery').

Key words and phrases

Bugger!	*Buggeration!*
Bugger me!	*What a bugger!*
Bugger off!	*(adjective) Bugger*
A bugger	*A bugger for*
Bugger about	*To bugger off*
Bugger on about	*Bugger something up*
Bugger all	*A bugger of a*
Be buggered	*Buggered if I know*
As buggery	*Like buggery!*

Exclamations and observations

Oh Bugger! Buggeration! Bugger it!

This is an exclamation used when the speaker has made a mistake or something has happened to irritate the speaker. It is not very strong in force so is not considered to be very vulgar (it is not as vulgar as 'balls!').

OH BUGGER! I CAN'T FIND MY KEYS

BUGGERATION! WHY DOES SOMETHING KEEP GOING WRONG WITH THE COMPUTER?

OH BUGGER IT! I'M NOT GOING TO THE PARTY. I'VE GOT NOTHING TO WEAR

Bugger me!

An exclamation of surprise.

> GUESS WHAT! YOU CAME
> FIRST IN THE EXAM...

> WELL, BUGGER ME!

What a bugger!

This is often an exclamation of sympathy when someone tells you about something that has gone wrong, or caused problems.

> I CAN'T GET ANY MONEY UNTIL THE
> BANKS OPEN ON MONDAY...

> WHAT A BUGGER!

Bugger off

This means go away but is not as forceful as 'fuck off' or 'piss off'.

> GO ON! BUGGER OFF! STOP
> ANNOYING ME!...

> BUT...

> I SAID BUGGER OFF!

A bugger

This word describes an unpleasant person.

> JOHN CAN BE A REAL BUGGER
> SOMETIMES

> DON'T BE A BUGGER!

A bugger for

This means very enthusiastic and energetic at doing something – though not necessarily approved of by the speaker.

> HE'S A BUGGER FOR ORGANIZING PARTIES

> HE'S A BUGGER FOR CHECKING EVERY DETAIL

Poor bugger!

A person who should be pitied, who needs sympathy.

> LOOK AT THAT MAN STANDING IN THE RAIN. POOR BUGGER!

> MY SON HAS BROKEN HIS LEG. THE POOR BUGGER WON'T BE ABLE TO PLAY FOOTBALL FOR A FEW MONTHS

Silly bugger!

Someone has done something stupid and you don't have much sympathy for him.

> THE SILLY BUGGER TRIED TO HIT A POLICEMAN!

> HE STOLE THE CAR TO IMPRESS HIS GIRLFRIEND. THE SILLY BUGGER!

Filthy bugger!

Someone who sees everything in the most disgusting sexual way – or who lives in a dirty way.

> HE'S A FILTHY BUGGER. HE ONLY HAS A BATH ONCE A MONTH

> HE'S A FILTHY BUGGER. ALL HE THINKS ABOUT IS SEX

Verb forms

Bugger about/around

This has the same meaning as 'fuck about/around' but is not so strong.

> STOP BUGGERING ABOUT AND DO SOME WORK!

> DON'T TAKE ANY NOTICE OF LINDA. SHE'S JUST BUGGERING AROUND

Bugger off

This means to leave a place quickly – generally to avoid a problem.

> I COULD SEE THAT THE PROBLEM WAS GOING TO GET WORSE SO I DECIDED TO BUGGER OFF

Bugger on about
This means to talk endlessly about nothing important.

> STOP BUGGERING ON ABOUT
> YOUR PERSONAL PROBLEMS. I'M NOT
> INTERESTED

> WHAT ARE YOU BUGGERING
> ON ABOUT?

Bugger (something) up
This means to make a mess of something. It has much the same meaning as 'fuck up' or 'balls up' but is not so forceful.

> JOHN HAS BUGGERED UP THE
> ARRANGEMENTS

> HE HAS BUGGERED THEM UP
> YET AGAIN!

Get (or be) buggered
To become broken or damaged. As a verb: to break or damage.

> HE BUGGERED THE COMPUTER

> THE COMPUTER GOT BUGGERED

Other forms
Bugger all
Like 'fuck all' this means: nothing.

> I WORKED REALLY HARD FOR
> HIM AND HE GAVE ME BUGGER ALL
> THANKS FOR IT

> WHAT BENEFIT DID I GET? NONE.
> ABSOLUTELY BUGGER ALL!

It's a bugger of a...

i) ... job!

This phrase is used to describe any long, difficult task or piece of work

> GETTING THE ROOF REPAIRED WAS A BUGGER OF A JOB!

> IT WAS A BUGGER OF A JOB REPAIRING THE RICE COOKER

ii) ...day!

This describes an unpleasant day

> IT WAS A BUGGER OF A DAY. I WAS ON THE TELEPHONE NON-STOP FROM 10AM TO 6PM

> WHAT A BUGGER OF A DAY! IT RAINED NON-STOP. I HOPE TOMORROW IS BETTER

iii)...car!

> IT'S A BUGGER OF A CAR. IT TAKES FOREVER TO GET IT GOING ON A COLD MORNING

Be buggered

This means to be exhausted, to be shattered, to have no energy left.

> WHEN HE CAME HOME HE LOOKED ABSOLUTELY BUGGERED

Be buggered if ...

This phrase means: I'm not going to do it.

> I'M BUGGERED IF I'M GOING TO
> GO OUT THIS EVENING. THE WEATHER
> IS TERRIBLE

> JAMES IS BUGGERED IF HE'S GOING
> TO APOLOGISE TO KEN. HE THINKS KEN
> SHOULD APOLOGISE TO HIM

Buggered if I know

This means to be completely ignorant.

> WHAT'S THE LARGEST CITY IN NEW
> ZEALAND?...

> I'M BUGGERED IF I KNOW

...as buggery

This is a phrase meaning 'extremely'.

> IT WAS HOT AS BUGGERY!

Like buggery!

A way of expressing strong disagreement.

> JOHN IS A REALLY GOOD GUY...

> LIKE BUGGERY! HE'S A REAL
> BASTARD SOMETIMES

Do something like buggery
This makes the action sound more energetic.

> **I WORKED LIKE BUGGERY TO FINISH THE PROJECT**

> **HE RAN LIKE BUGGERY ALL THE WAY HOME**

Sod
This means the same as bugger. It is short for sodomite (i.e. someone from the Biblical city of Sodom, a place famous for all sorts of perversions and debauchery). This is an old fashioned insulting word for homosexual. Nowadays only the shortened form 'sod' is used.

Key words and phrases

Sod it!	*Sod off!*	*Sodding*
Be a sod	*Sod all*	*Sod's law*
Odds and sods		

Sod it!
This exclamation signals that the speaker has finally come to a decision, often one that he doesn't like.

> **OH SOD IT! I SUPPOSE I'LL HAVE TO DO SOME WORK.**

> **OH SOD IT! I'M FED UP WITH THIS JOB. I'M GOING TO DO SOMETHING ELSE.**

Sod off

This is a way of saying 'go away'. It isn't very aggressive.

> **JUST SOD OFF, WILL YOU. LEAVE ME ALONE. I DON'T WANT TO TALK TO YOU**

Sodding

This is used as a word that adds negative emphasis.

> **WHERE'S THE SODDING BUS?**

> **WHAT A SODDING DAY! I'LL BE GLAD TO GET HOME**

> **SODDING HELL! I'M LATE**

A sod

This just means someone is not very nice. It is less strong than bugger.

> **DON'T BE A SOD**

> **YOU CAN BE A REAL SOD SOMETIMES, CAN'T YOU?**

Sod all

Nothing.

> **WHAT DID HE GIVE YOU?...**

> **SOD ALL! NOT A PENNY**

Sod's Law

Sod's Law goes like this: If something bad can go wrong it will go wrong. This is also referred to as Murphy's Law.

EVERYTHING I DID TO TRY AND IMPRESS HER WENT WRONG...

IT'S SOD'S LAW!

Odds and Sods

This phrase means miscellaneous items.

PUT THE BOOKS IN THIS BOX AND ALL THE OTHER ODDS AND SODS IN THE OTHER BOX

THE FUCKING FUCKER'S FUCKING FUCKED THE FUCKER UP

THE 'F' WORD —————

This is the most common of all the swear words. It's almost impossible to avoid it. It appears as graffiti on walls, you can find it on tee shirts. Now, there is even a chain of shops whose name makes a play on the word: FCUK – French Connection United Kingdom. They make a sweet alcoholic drink called FCUK Spirit. What do you say when you want to order one in a bar?

Fuck is the absolute and complete vulgarity. Perhaps for this reason, it is the swear word with the widest range of meanings attached to it. The main meaning of fuck is to have sexual intercourse. But while making love is such a nice thing to do, the word 'fuck' makes the act sound ugly. It is an aggressive word. This is something it shares with related words in German, Dutch and Swedish which, in addition to sex, carry the meaning of 'to strike' or 'to thrust' or 'to move back and forth'. Read Jesse Sheidlower's "The F-Word" for further details of the word's history.

Let us now look at the many ways in which the word is commonly used.

Key words and phrases

Exclamations:
For fuck's sake!, fuck!, fucking hell!, fuck it!, fuck me!,
fuck no!, fuck somebody!, fuck something!, fuck that!,
fuck this shit!, like fuck!, the fuck!, what the fuck!,
well fuck a duck!

Instructions:
Fuck off!, get fucked!, go fuck yourself!

Adding emphasis:
Fucking, fucking well, a fuck of a, the fuck.

Nouns & Noun phrases:
Fuck, fuck all, sweet F.A, fucker, fuckwit (fuckhead etc).

Verb or verb phrase:
To fuck, to be fucked, to fuck the brains /
shit out of (someone), to fuck about,
to fuck around, to give someone the fuck around,
to fuck away, to fuck off, to fuck over, to fuck up,
to fuck somebody up, to fuck with, to give a fuck.

Adjectives:
Can't be fucked to, fucked, fuckable, fuckheaded, fuck-me,
fucked off, fucked out, fucksome (wench).

Others:
For the fuck of it, fuckaholic, fuckathon, fuckery, fucking A,
fuckloads, fuckster / fuckstress, fuckstrated, good fuck,
hurts like fuck, like fuck.

Euphemisms:
Flipping, freaking, frigging, the f word.

Variations:
Effing, motherfucker, motherfucking.

Exclamations

For fuck's sake!

This is an extreme way of saying 'for God's sake' or 'for Christ's sake'. It can also be written as one word.

Fuck!

You've just discovered something bad, or you've just done something stupid, or you've just remembered something awful. This is the exclamation you hear everywhere. It is often used with the sound 'Oh' in front.

Fucking Hell!

This is an expression of anger – and is more angry than 'bloody hell'.

> FUCKING HELL! WHERE ARE MY SHOES?

> FUCKING HELL! WHY DIDN'T YOU TELL ME THE TRUTH EARLIER?

> FUCKING HELL! IT WASN'T MY FAULT!

Fuck it!

This can mean 'I have had enough of (something)' and I just want to finish with it.

> OH FUCK IT! I'M QUITTING MY JOB

> OH FUCK IT. LET'S GO

Fuck me!

This is usually said as an expression of great surprise.

> JOHN AND JANE HAVE DECIDED TO GET MARRIED...

> WELL, FUCK ME! THAT IS A SURPRISE. I DIDN'T KNOW THEY WERE THAT SERIOUS

Fuck no!

This phrase is usually spoken with force suggesting a kind of horror at the thought.

> DID YOU TELL JOHN THE NEWS?...

> FUCK NO! SOMEONE ELSE CAN TELL HIM!

Fuck you! Fuck him! etc.

You're angry with someone. Very angry.

I DON'T THINK WE SHOULD ANNOY JACK...

WELL, FUCK YOU! I DON'T CARE WHAT YOU THINK...

YEAH, FUCK JACK

JOHN TOLD JANE WHAT YOU SAID...

WELL, FUCK JOHN! THAT'S THE LAST TIME I TELL HIM ANYTHING

Fuck...

Here, fuck means 'I don't want to have anything to do with (something). You can keep it.'

FUCK WORK, LET'S PARTY!

FUCK EXERCISE. I'M GOING HOME TO WATCH TELEVISION AND HAVE A FEW BEERS

FUCK THE WORLD, I WANT TO GET OFF

FUCK THE JOB. I'M QUITTING

FUCK THE MEETING. I'M NOT GOING

Fuck that!

This shows complete rejection of what somebody else is saying. A slightly stronger version is 'Fuck that for a lark' and another is 'fuck this for a game of soldiers!'

Fuck this shit!

This phrase expresses strong feelings of anger and rejection for something.

Like fuck!

A way of expressing disagreement or refusal. It's a strong way of saying 'like hell'.

The fuck...!
This is used when responding angrily or very negatively
with short answers.

> I EXPECT YOU WILL BE AT
> THE PARTY...

> THE FUCK I WILL! I HAVEN'T
> BEEN INVITED

> YOU'VE GOT A GREAT CAR...

> THE FUCK I HAVE. IT WOULDN'T
> START THIS MORNING

Well, fuck a duck!
An expression of surprise.

> WELL, FUCK A DUCK! IT'S JOHN! I
> HAVEN'T SEEN YOU FOR AGES

Instructions

Fuck off!!
This means 'go away' or 'get away from me'. Or it can mean
'No!!' It is forceful.

> CAN YOU GIVE ME SOME MONEY?...

> NO. JUST FUCK OFF

Get fucked!

This is a strong instruction to go away or face the consequences. Or if said in a friendly context it might just mean you've just said something really silly. It can be made strong by adding the words 'go and...' in front.

Go fuck yourself!

This is a very crude way of saying 'go away, stop bothering me'.

Emphasis

Fucking...

This is one of the most common ways in which 'fuck' is used in normal speech. It adds a strong negative meaning to the sentence.

i) *'fucking'* can be put immediately before any noun to express some kind of displeasure or unhappiness with that person or thing:

THE FUCKING WAITER REFUSED TO SERVE ME

I WAITED HALF AN HOUR FOR THE FUCKING BUS

THE FUCKING TELEVISION WOULDN'T WORK

THE FUCKING WATER WAS FREEZING

ii) We can put *'fucking'* immediately in front of verbs too. When we do this, it merely adds a kind of emphasis to the message.

I AM NOT FUCKING GOING ANYWHERE

THE DOG FUCKING ATE ALL THE STEAKS

WHY AM I DOING THIS? I CAN'T EVEN FUCKING SWIM

iii) We can also put *'fucking'* immediately in front of adjectives and adverbs for the same purpose, to add strength to the message. Notice that it doesn't necessarily have a negative meaning. It can also be used to add force to positive messages.

iv) *'Fucking'* can also be used to add force to commands and orders.

But it is more common with negative imperatives.

What a fucking...!

This is a phrase that generally suggests extreme exasperation with something.

> WHAT A FUCKING STUPID IDEA!

> WHAT A FUCKING AWFUL DAY!

> WHAT A FUCKING BORING MEETING THAT WAS!

But it can also express the opposite - something that is very good.

> WHAT A FUCKING BRILLIANT IDEA!

> WHAT A FUCKING GREAT JOB HE'S GOT

> WHAT A FUCKING WONDERFUL PARTY THAT WAS LAST NIGHT

Fucking well...

Adds emphasis.

> I'M NOT GOING TO THE PARTY...

> OH YES, YOU FUCKING WELL ARE

> I'M GOING TO TELL JOHN WHAT YOU TOLD ME...

> OH NO YOU FUCKING WELL WON'T

A fuck of a...

This phrase is used to add negative emphasis.

> I HAD A FUCK OF A TIME GETTING HERE.
> MY CAR KEPT BREAKING DOWN

> THE OFFICE WAS IN A FUCK OF A MESS

> I'VE HAD A FUCK OF A DAY. WHAT I
> NEED NOW IS A LONG HOT BATH!

...the fuck...!

This phrase is used to add emphasis to a very small number of orders that require immediate action. The words 'the fuck' come between the verb and the preposition.

> SHUT THE FUCK UP!

> GET THE FUCK OUT OF MY WAY!

What the fuck...?

Do you remember all those questions that were made more forceful by adding 'the hell' (e.g. What the hell do you want?). Well, they can be made even more forceful by replacing 'hell' with 'fuck'.

> WHAT THE FUCK DO I CARE?

> WHO THE FUCK DO YOU THINK YOU ARE?

> HOW THE FUCK ARE WE GOING TO
> RAISE THE MONEY WE NEED TO START
> THE BUSINESS?

> **WHERE THE FUCK DID YOU BUY THAT HAT?**

> **WHEN THE FUCK ARE YOU GOING TO BE READY?**

Sometimes, to express shock and disbelief, you might say: *'What the fuck...?'* And not finish the question. Just leave the words hanging in the air.

We can also say *'what the fuck'* in the same way as we said 'what the hell' meaning 'OK I'll do (something) though I'm not very excited about doing it'.

> **OK, WHAT THE FUCK, IF YOU WANT TO CLIMB THAT MOUNTAIN, I'LL COME WITH YOU**

Noun or noun phrases

Fuck

An insulting way of referring to a person.

> **HE'S A DUMB FUCK**

> **THERE WERE TWO FUCKS STANDING OUTSIDE THE SHOP**

Fuck

This word 'the most famous of all the' 4 letter words, first appeared in 1278 as the name of a man 'John le Fucker'. It is not known why he had this name! It didn't otherwise appear in English until after 1500. It has been suggested that it is either of German or Scandinavian origin. Norwegian dialect has fukka meaning to copulate. Swedish has focka also meaning to copulate but, in addition, meaning 'to hit'. This aggressive meaning is still very much part of the present use of the modern English use of fuck.

This means 'nothing'. It is sometimes used with the word 'sweet' (sweet fuck all). Also sometimes the speaker will just say the initials: 'F.A'.

It can also be used in a statement - usually expressing the level of knowledge (none) about a subject.

Fuck all I care

This phrase is used sometimes to mean: I don't care at all.

FUCK ALL JOHN CARES WHETHER I PASS THE EXAM OR NOT

FUCK ALL I CARE IF SHE PREFERS TO IGNORE ME

Fucker

This is a word you can use about someone you don't like. It suggests that the other person is not to be trusted.

YOU'RE A FUCKER, DO YOU KNOW THAT?

Fuckwit etc

This is a rude way of saying someone is stupid.

JOHN CAN BE A COMPLETE FUCKWIT SOMETIMES

Verb or verb phrase

To fuck or be fucked

Sex can be used to express power as well as love. It is this sense of the word that is used here: the idea of dominance, of beating someone, of winning and making someone else lose badly or of being badly defeated in some way.

> HE FUCKED ME TOTALLY

> HE THOUGHT HE WOULD BEAT ME BUT I FUCKED HIM

> DON'T MESS WITH ME OR I'LL FUCK YOU!

> MY BOSS HEARD ME MAKING FUN OF HIM. THAT HAS FUCKED MY CHANCES OF BEING PROMOTED

Fuck the brains out of someone.
Fuck the living shit out of someone

These two phrases are boasts of aggressive sexual activity.

> I FUCKED THE BRAINS OUT OF HER. IT WAS BLOODY MARVELOUS!

> I FUCKED THE LIVING SHIT OUT OF HER!

The second phrase also can be used to describe physically attacking and hitting someone.

> IF YOU MESS WITH ME I'LL FUCK THE LIVING SHIT OUT OF YOU!

To fuck around

To have sex with a lot of people.

> SHE'S PREGNANT BUT SHE DOESN'T
> KNOW WHO THE FATHER IS...

> I'M NOT SURPRISED. SHE'S BEEN
> FUCKING AROUND FOR A LONG TIME

To fuck around/about (with)

To play with something in a silly way, to not take something seriously. It can be used without an object (to fuck around.) or with an object (to fuck around with something).

> JOHN'S NOT DOING ANYTHING IMPORTANT.
> HE'S JUST FUCKING AROUND

> STOP FUCKING AROUND WITH
> MY COMPUTER

> WHY DON'T YOU STOP FUCKING ABOUT
> AND GET YOURSELF A GOOD JOB

> DON'T FUCK ABOUT
> WITH ME

To fuck (someone) around.
To give someone the fuck around

To cause problems for someone, to be unhelpful.

> *I WISH YOU WOULD STOP FUCKING ME AROUND*

> *HE PRETENDED HE WAS TRYING TO HELP BUT HE JUST GAVE ME THE FUCK AROUND ALL AFTERNOON*

To fuck away

To waste.

> *HIS FATHER LEFT HIM A LOT OF MONEY BUT HE JUST FUCKED IT AWAY AND NOW HE HASN'T GOT A CENT*

To fuck off (1)

To go away.

> *HE DIDN'T WANT ME TO STAY SO I FUCKED OFF*

To fuck off (2)

This means to be lazy or to avoid doing work.

> *JOHN NEVER DOES HIS SHARE OF THE WORK. HE'S ALWAYS FUCKING OFF SOMEWHERE*

To fuck someone over

To cause someone harm – usually physically.

> *WE GOT INTO AN ARGUMENT AND THEN HE STARTED HITTING ME. HE REALLY FUCKED ME OVER*

To fuck up

To make a mess of something, to do it badly.

> **I FUCKED UP THE JOB INTERVIEW SO I DON'T THINK THEY'LL OFFER ME THE JOB**

To fuck someone up

To harm someone psychologically. This is related to the adjective form: be fucked up (be psychologically harmed) and the noun form: a fuck up (a person who is a psychological mess).

> **HIS PARENTS REALLY FUCKED HIM UP**

> **HE'S REALLY FUCKED UP**

> **HE'S A COMPLETE FUCK UP**

To fuck with...

This is an aggressive phrase meaning to do something that is intended to cause problems.

> **DON'T FUCK WITH ME! KEEP OUT OF MY WAY! DO YOU UNDERSTAND?**

> **HE TRIED TO FUCK WITH THE ARRANGEMENTS BUT I STOPPED THAT**

Give a fuck...

Generally used in the negative (I don't give a fuck) – it is a more forceful way of saying 'don't give a damn' this means 'don't care'. Sometimes it is given added emphasis by adding the word 'flying'.

Adjectives and adjective phrases

Can't be fucked (to do something)

This is the vulgar form of the phrase 'can't be bothered'. That means you don't have the interest or the energy to do something.

Fucked

For things, this means broken or unusable. For people, it means ruined or destroyed.

JOHN IS FUCKED! HE'S CERTAINLY GOING TO LOSE HIS JOB

THE CAR WON'T START. IT'S OLD AND IT'S COMPLETELY FUCKED

OH FUCK! NOW WE'RE REALLY FUCKED!

IRAQ HAS NUCLEAR BOMB!!

Feel fucked

This should feel good, but it doesn't. In this sense fucked means exhausted or very ill or totally drunk and incapacitated.

I'VE HAD TOO MUCH TO DRINK. I FEEL TOTALLY FUCKED

I'VE JUST RUN A MARATHON AND I FEEL COMPLETELY FUCKED

Fuckable

This is an adjective to describe a person who is considered to be attractive.

LOOK AT HER! SHE'S FUCKABLE!

Fuckheaded

Stupid or obstinate.

JOHN CAN BE REALLY FUCKHEADED SOMETIMES

Fuck-me

This phrase can be used as an adjective to describe clothes that a girl or woman might wear to make her look attractive. This can also appear as come-fuck-me.

SHE PUT ON HER FUCK-ME SHOES AND WENT OUT

SHE LOOKED AT ME WITH HER COME-FUCK-ME EXPRESSION AND I WENT WEAK AT THE KNEES.

Fucked off

To be angry.

I FEEL REALLY FUCKED OFF THAT I WASN'T INVITED TO THE PARTY

I'M REALLY FUCKED OFF ABOUT THE WAY HE IGNORED ME YESTERDAY!

Fucked out
To be physically exhausted by having had too much sex.

> WE'VE BEEN SHAGGING ALL DAY. I'M COMPLETELY FUCKED OUT

Fucksome wench
This is a rhyming pun on another phrase – 'buxom wench' – meaning a woman with large breasts. Here it would mean a girl that the speaker would like to have sex with.

> SHE'S A FUCKSOME WENCH!

Miscellaneous

For the fuck of it
Just for fun or just because I felt like it.

> I DECIDED TO GO TO PARIS – JUST FOR THE FUCK OF IT

Fuckaholic
A person addicted to sex.

> JOHN IS A FUCKAHOLIC. HE CAN'T STOP CHASING WOMEN

Fuckathon
A long sex session requiring stamina.

> SUSY IS A REAL GOER. WE HAD A FUCKATHON ALL SATURDAY AFTERNOON

Fuckery
Nonsense.

> ENOUGH OF THIS FUCKERY. LET'S GET SERIOUS

Fucking A
Very good.

> HEY JOHN! DID I TELL YOU? I PASSED THE EXAM...

> HEY! FUCKING A! THAT'S GREAT

Fuckloads
A lot of something.

> WE HAD TO STAY LATE AT THE OFFICE. WE HAD FUCKLOADS OF WORK TO DO

> HE'S NOT POOR. HIS FATHER'S GOT FUCKLOADS OF MONEY

Fuckster / fuckstress
A fuckster is a sexually promiscuous man and a fuckstress is a similar woman.

> JOHN IS A BIT OF A FUCKSTER

> SUSY IS A REAL FUCKSTRESS

Fuckstrated
To feel sexually frustrated because one isn't getting enough sex.

> I FEEL REALLY FUCKSTRATED!

Goat fuck

A complete mess.

> JOHN MADE A COMPLETE GOAT
> FUCK OF THE ARRANGEMENTS

Good fuck

This means good in bed.

> YOU SHOULD TRY HIM. HE'S A GOOD FUCK

Hurts like fuck

Hurts badly.

> MY LEG HURTS LIKE FUCK

Like fuck!

This phrase is a way of stating that some supposed fact is untrue. Other phrases that have the same meaning are: Like hell! Like buggery!

> JOHN SAYS HE WENT OUT WITH
> MARY LAST NIGHT...

> LIKE FUCK HE DID. SHE WAS
> WITH ME ALL EVENING

Mindfuck

A state of confusion (often drug induced).

> *I WAS IN A COMPLETE MINDFUCK. I DIDN'T KNOW WHAT I WAS DOING*

Euphemisms for 'fuck'

The word fuck is so strong that even its euphemisms can be strong enough to cause offence. Historically the following words were sometimes used in novels instead of fuck: fug, frig, feck. But nowadays only 'flaming', 'flipping', 'frigging' or 'freaking' may still be heard – generally as intensifiers: for example in the phrase 'flipping hell!'. However, the increasing acceptability of 'fuck' has meant that these euphemisms are being used less and less. However, if people wish to refer to the word without using it they may say 'the F-word'.

> *OH FLIP. I CAN'T FIND MY KEY*

> *FLIPPING HELL!*

> *HE SAID A LOT OF BAD WORDS. HE USED THE F-WORD THREE OR FOUR TIMES*

> *IT'S FREAKING COLD!*

> *DON'T FRIGGING LIE TO ME! TELL ME THE TRUTH!*

> *YOU ARE BEING A FLAMING NUISANCE. GO AWAY AND LEAVE ME ALONE*

Variations on fuck

Effing

Effing can be used instead of fucking, where it is used to add emphasis.

PASS ME THE EFFING SCREWDRIVER

I WAS STOPPED BY THE EFFING POLICE

Effing is also often used as part of the phrase *'effing and blinding'* – which is a euphemism for using bad language.

THE CUSTOMER GOT REALLY ANGRY AND STARTED EFFING AND BLINDING. I HAD TO TELL HIM TO MIND HIS LANGUAGE

Motherfucker

This is an Americanism and is normally only used in two forms a) as a direct insult to someone or b) as a negative comment about someone. Motherfucker means the same as 'fucker'.

> *YOU MOTHERFUCKER!*

> *HE'S A MOTHERFUCKER*

Motherfucking:

This is used in the same way as 'fucking' before a noun but is not used to emphasise verbs or adjectives.

> *YOU'RE A MOTHERFUCKING BASTARD!*

WHERE ARE THE MOTHERFUCKING POLICE WHEN YOU NEED THEM?

Snafu

a war-time phrase that is still used but is old fashioned. Pronounced 'sna-foo', it is an acronym standing for:

<u>S</u>ituation <u>N</u>ormal <u>A</u>ll <u>F</u>ucked <u>U</u>p.

SCREW

This word has the same meaning as fuck but it is only a little bit less ugly so it doesn't really count as a euphemism. Some uses have been given on page 115.

Key words and phrases

Screw you	*Screw that*
To get screwed	*To screw around*
To screw up	

Screw... !

This is an angry way of dismissing the importance of somebody or something.

SCREW YOU!

SCREW THE MEETING. I'M NOT GOING

SCREW JOHN. I'M NOT WAITING FOR HIM

Screw that!

This is a phrase which is used when someone is annoyed and refuses to co-operate with a suggested action or activity.

MARY WANTS YOU TO BE NICE TO SUSAN...

SCREW THAT! I'M NEVER GOING TO TALK TO HER AGAIN

> YOU'RE GOING TO HAVE TO GET
> YOUR HAIR CUT SOON...

> SCREW THAT! I'LL HAVE MY HAIR
> AS LONG AS I WANT

To screw someone / to get screwed by someone

This has the idea of cheating someone, or ripping someone off.

> I TRIED TO DO SOME BUSINESS WITH
> HIM BUT I GOT REALLY SCREWED

> IF YOU TRY TO SCREW ME, I'LL
> MAKE SURE IT'S THE LAST THING
> YOU EVER DO

Screw around

This has the same two meanings as fuck around – both having sex with a lot of people and not taking things seriously.

> DON'T SCREW AROUND WITH THAT MACHINE.
> IT'S WORTH A LOT OF MONEY

> SHE USED TO SCREW AROUND A
> LOT BUT NOW SHE'S BEEN GOING OUT WITH
> JOHN FOR OVER A YEAR

To screw up / to screw something up
This has the same meaning as 'fuck up'.

> I SCREWED UP THE INTERVIEW SO I DON'T THINK THEY WILL OFFER ME THE JOB

> YOU MADE A MESS OF THE EXAM LAST YEAR SO DON'T SCREW UP AGAIN THIS YEAR

SHAG

To be shagged / to be shagged out
To be exhausted.

> I'VE BEEN WALKING NOW FOR TEN HOURS. I'M COMPLETELY SHAGGED OUT

> I FEEL COMPLETELY SHAGGED

INSULTS AND ANGRY WORDS

Expressing anger directly at a person

Sometimes we get very angry with someone face to face – and we might 'call them names':

Key words and phrases

Shit!	*Cunt!*	*Bastard!*
Prick!	*Son-of-a-bitch!*	*Dickhead!*

YOU SHIT!

YOU CUNT!

YOU BASTARD!

HE'S A STUPID PRICK!

JOHN IS A SON-OF-A-BITCH!

HE'S A DICKHEAD

If we want to make it a bit stronger we might add intensifying words.

Intensifiers

Fucking	*Lump of (shit)*	*Complete*
Absolute	*Real*	*Right*
Total		

Go away! I don't like you.
I don't want to talk to you!
I'm angry with you!
Key words and phrases

Not vulgar:
*Get lost!, take a hike!, go take a running jump!,
on your bike!, beat it!, buzz off!, go away!,
stop bothering me!*

Slightly vulgar:
*Go to hell!, get knotted!, get stuffed!, up yours!, naff off!,
bog off!*

Very vulgar:
*Fuck you!, screw you!, bugger you!, up your bum!,
go fuck yourself!, shove it up your arse!, get stuffed!,
stick it up your arse!, fuck off!, sod off!, bugger off!,
get out of my face!, get the fuck out of my way!, piss off!,
get your arse out of here!, get your arse out of my face!*

WILL YOU LEND ME SOME MONEY?...

NO, I WON'T. NOW, PISS OFF!

I THINK YOU SHOULD GO HOME NOW...

SOD OFF! I DON'T WANT TO TALK TO YOU

I JUST WANT TO BE YOUR FRIEND...

GO AWAY! LEAVE ME ALONE. JUST BUZZ OFF!

It's Bad

Sometimes we want to say that something (eg. a restaurant or film) is bad.

Key words and phrases

Bloody awful	*Godawful*	*Grotty*
Manky	*Piss awful*	*The pits*
Sucks	*Stinks*	

THIS SITUATION STINKS!

THE FILM SUCKS!

THE PARTY WAS GODAWFUL!

THIS PLACE IS THE PITS!

WHAT A PISS AWFUL DAY IT HAS BEEN!

THIS PLACE IS REALLY MANKY. IT LOOKS DISGUSTING AND IT SMELLS AWFUL.

HE LIVES IN A GROTTY HOUSE

That's nonsense!

It is very common for people to have disagreements – and to express, in a vulgar way, their contempt for the other person's point of view. Here are some ways of expressing aggressive disagreement.

Key words and phrases

> **Not vulgar:**
> *Codswallop, baloney, bunkum, bunk, hooey*
> *talk through (one's) hat.*
>
> **Less vulgar:**
> *BS, hogwash, horse manure, bull.*
>
> **More vulgar:**
> *Crap, shit, balls, bollocks, bullshit, horseshit.*

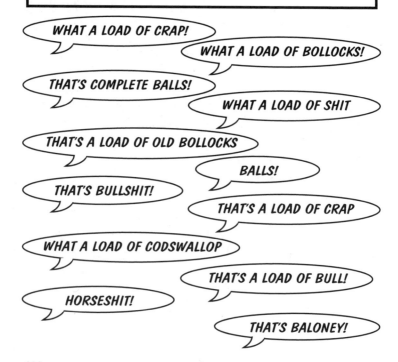

WHAT A LOAD OF CRAP!

WHAT A LOAD OF BOLLOCKS!

THAT'S COMPLETE BALLS!

WHAT A LOAD OF SHIT

THAT'S A LOAD OF OLD BOLLOCKS

BALLS!

THAT'S BULLSHIT!

THAT'S A LOAD OF CRAP

WHAT A LOAD OF CODSWALLOP

THAT'S A LOAD OF BULL!

HORSESHIT!

THAT'S BALONEY!

THAT'S COMPLETE BUNKUM

THAT'S A LOAD OF HOGWASH!

YOU'RE TALKING THROUGH YOUR HAT!

Being dismissive

We use these phrases when we wish to reject something completely. There's no point in discussing it further!

Key words and phrases

Sod that!	*Bugger that!*	*Fuck that!*
Balls to that!	*Stuff it!*	

JOHN SAYS TO WAIT FOR HIM...

BUGGER THAT. I'M GOING OUT NOW!

JOHN THINKS YOU SHOULD APOLOGISE TO MARY...

SOD THAT! I'VE GOT NOTHING TO APOLOGISE FOR

AREN'T YOU GOING TO HELP ME WASH THE DISHES?...

BALLS TO THAT! I'M GOING OUT!

Telling people to go away.

What he would like to say:

What he actually says:

GET THE FUCK OUT OF MY WAY YOU ARSEHOLE

EXCUSE ME. YOU'RE IN MY WAY

Contemptible people
Key words

Slightly vulgar:
Berk, plonker, jerk, stinker, knob, pillock.

Very vulgar:
Tosser, wanker, scumbag, scuzz bucket, arsehole, dirtbag, douche bag, shithead*, dipstick, cocksucker, minger (minger is pronounced ming-er).

*Note: Many other insults can be produced by combining a rude word: Eg: **fuck, shit, piss, dick** etc. with one of the following words: ...**face**, ...**brain**, ...**head** and ...**bag**.

HE'S A COMPLETE BERK!

HE'S A STUPID PILLOCK

HE'S AN ABSOLUTE JERK!

HE'S SUCH A PLONKER!

HE'S A TOSSER!

The man (or woman) is very stupid!

Stupidity is a cause of a great deal of anger – other people's stupidity! It is one of the easiest insults to throw at someone.

Key words

> *Slightly vulgar:*
> Chucklehead, dope, git, klutz, nincompoop, numbskull, Schlemiel, schmuck, cretin, moron, blockhead, chump, nit, dimwit, dodo, dummy, twit, ninny, right Charlie, dork, brain donor.
>
> ---
>
> *Very vulgar:*
> Dumb fuck, dumb shit, dumb ass, fuckwit, have shit for brains.

DON'T BE A KLUTZ

HE'S A NIT

YOU'RE A SCHMUCK

HE'S A COMPLETE DIMWIT

Here are some other ways of describing someone who really is not very intelligent.

(*Note: in old money, 'bob' was slang for shilling and 'quid' is short for pound. There used to be 20 shillings in a pound).

That man (or woman) is crazy!

This is one of the most popular type of insults. Here are some of the most common words – none of them is really vulgar:

Key words

> **Adjectives:**
> Bats, bonkers, loony, whacko, barmy.
>
> ---
>
> **Phrases:**
> Off (one's) trolley, round the bend, round the twist.
>
> ---
>
> **Nouns:**
> Dingbat, freak, freakazoid, fruitcake, kook, nutcase, nutter, oddball, screwball, weirdo, basketcase.

(*Note: this expression means 'some mothers have idiots for children – and here's an example!')

YOU'RE TOTALLY OFF YOUR TROLLEY!

HE'S COMPLETELY ROUND THE BEND!

SHE'S BATS!

HE'S A BIT OF AN ODDBALL

SHE'S ROUND THE TWIST!

HE'S A COMPLETE FRUITCAKE!

SHE'S A TOTAL DINGBAT!

HE'S A TOTAL WHACKO

HE'S A REAL FREAKAZOID

WHAT DO YOU THINK OF HIM?

WELL, HE'S CERTAINLY DIFFERENT

SCREWBALL, FRUITCAKE, LOONY, NUTTER

Uncultured people

US:
Hick, redneck.
British:
Peasant, yokel.

People who are easily tricked
Key words

Sucker	*Patsy*	*Mug*

DON'T SIGN THE CONTRACT. YOU'RE A SUCKER IF YOU DO

I AGREED TO TAKE THE BLAME FOR HIS MISTAKE. I WAS A REAL PATSY

DON'T BE A MUG

Yes-man

Yes-men are the people who like to agree with everything their boss says. In doing this, they hope their boss will help their careers. However, they are not popular with other people.

Key words **and phrases**

An arse licker	*Ass kisser*
A suck up	*To suck up*
A brown nose	*A butt sucker*
To suck butt	

YOU'VE BECOME A REAL ARSE LICKER

WHY DO YOU ALWAYS SUCK UP TO THE BOSS?

BEING A BROWN NOSE WON'T DO YOU ANY GOOD

I DON'T LIKE HIM. HE'S A REAL ASS KISSER

TO GET AHEAD IN THIS JOB YOU ARE GOING TO HAVE TO SUCK SOME BUTT

Good talker

Some people like to talk and talk and talk – on every subject under the sun. They know everything.

Key words

Windbag	Bullshitter	Smartarse
Smart alec	Clever dick	Know it all

DON'T BE SUCH A SMARTARSE!

DON'T LISTEN TO HIM. HE'S JUST A BULLSHITTER

JOHN'S ALL RIGHT BUT HE CAN BE A BIT IF A WINDBAG SOMETIMES

I DON'T LIKE SMART ALECS

YOU CAN'T TALK TO BILL. HE'S A KNOW IT ALL

Lazy or generally useless person

People who are useless, who pretend to be useful but aren't and people who waste our time, have the ability to make us very angry.

Key words

> **Not vulgar:**
> Deadhead, loser, stoner, time waster.
>
> **Vulgar:**
> Jerk off, lame dick, plonker, tosser, wanker.

HE'S A LOSER

HE'S A LAME DICK

HE'S A STONER

JUST IGNORE HIM. HE'S A TOTAL JERK OFF!

WHY ARE YOU SUCH A PLONKER SOMETIMES?

DON'T HAVE ANYTHING TO DO WITH HIM. HE'S A COMPLETE TIME WASTER

WHAT A WANKER!

HE'LL NEVER STICK WITH A JOB. HE'S A REAL DEADHEAD

Animals

Sometimes we insult people by suggesting they are like certain animals.

He's a rat: untrustworthy, despicable person.

He's a louse: despicable person.

He's a worm: disgusting, weak, despicable person.

He's a pig: greedy person with no manners – often used of men who have little respect for women: 'chauvinist pig'

He's a slimy snake: untrustworthy person.

He's an ass: stupid person. Here ass is another name for donkey.

Atomic mutton: an older woman trying to look like a young, sexy girl.

Insulting women
Key words

Not vulgar:
Bimbo, gold digger, silly cow, silly moo, old bat, old bag.

Less vulgar:
Bitch, bean flicker, slut, scrubber, slapper, whore, tramp, hussy, slag, trollop.

Very vulgar:
Cunt.

Adjective:
Slutty.

Specifically American
Noun:
Ho (hoe).

Adjective:
Skanky.

Bimbo

A woman who is young, beautiful and stupid.

> SHE'S JUST A STUPID BIMBO

Gold digger

A woman who is only after one thing – money!

> SHE'S A GOLD DIGGER

Bean flicker

Lesbian.

Slut etc.

But the most vulgar words suggest a mixture of sexual availability, unattractiveness and dirty personal habits.

> SHE'S A SLUT

> SHE'S A SLUTTY BITCH

> SHE'S A SKANKY BITCH

> SHE'S A SCRUBBER

> SHE'S NOTHING BUT A TRAMP

> SHE'S A WHORE

> SHE'S BEGINNING TO LOOK LIKE AN OLD SLAG

Some women just can't stop going out with men who are bad for them.

> SHE'S A WHORE FOR PUNISHMENT

Or if she's just stupid, we might say:

> **SHE'S A SILLY COW**

> **SHE'S A SILLY MOO**

Old bag, Old bat

an insulting way of referring to an unattractive or otherwise
unpleasant woman – usually quite old.

> **DON'T WORRY ABOUT THE LANDLADY.
> SHE'S JUST AN OLD BAG**

> **SHE'S AN OLD BAT**

A dog

An ugly woman.

> **SHE'S A REAL DOG**

Cunt!

This is the most vulgar way of referring to a woman in an
insulting way.

> **SHE'S A CUNT! I DON'T LIKE HER**

Slag off

A slag is a foul-mouthed woman. To slag someone off is
to curse and swear at someone (usually for doing
something you don't like). It can be used for both sexes.

> **HE SLAGGED ME OFF FOR PARKING
> IN FRONT OF HIS HOUSE**

BITCH

Literally, this word means a female dog but it is more commonly used to refer to a woman who is unfriendly or aggressive.

SHE'S A REAL BITCH

But it can also be used in the following ways:

Bitch!	Tough/hard bitch	Bitchy
Bitch (on) about	...is a bitch	
Son of a bitch (s.o.b.)	Door bitch	

Bitch!

i) This is an exclamation when something has gone wrong.

BITCH! I'VE BURNT MY HAND

ii) A bitch is a person, usually female or an effeminate man, who says bad things about people behind their backs or who tries to harm people's reputations. Or someone who enjoys saying nasty things about people.

DON'T TRUST HER. SHE CAN BE A REAL BITCH

Tough bitch / Hard bitch

A tough woman who is not easily dominated might be described like this:

SHE'S A TOUGH BITCH

SHE'S A HARD BITCH

Bitch

This is an old English word meaning 'female dog'. It has been used as a derogatory word referring to women for at least 600 years.

Bitchy

This is the adjective form.

> I CAN SEE WHY HIS WIFE LEFT HIM FOR ANOTHER MAN...

> OH! YOU ARE BITCHY!

> SHE CAN BE QUITE BITCHY SOMETIMES

> THAT'S A REALLY BITCHY THING TO SAY

Bitching / bitching on about

The action of saying bad things about somebody or something – or complaining about them.

> I CAN'T BEAR TO TALK TO JOHN FOR LONG. HE'S ALWAYS BITCHING ABOUT ONE THING OR ANOTHER

> STOP BITCHING ON ABOUT YOUR JOB. IF YOU DON'T LIKE IT GET ANOTHER ONE

...is a bitch

This is used in a general sense meaning something is bad.

> LIFE'S A BITCH

> NOT HAVING A CAR IS A REAL BITCH

Son-of-a-bitch

This phrase can be used as an insult, or as an expression of anger at someone.

> **YOU SON OF A BITCH**

> **JOHN CAN BE A REAL SON-OF-A-BITCH SOMETIMES**

It can also be used as an adjective.

> **I CAN'T MAKE THIS SON-OF-A-BITCH CAR START. I DON'T KNOW WHAT'S WRONG**

'Son-of-a-bitch!' can also be used as an expression of anger.

> **SON-OF-A-BITCH! I'VE CUT MY FINGER**

S.o.b

This is a polite way of saying son of a bitch.

> **YOU'RE BEING A REAL S.O.B.**

Other possible meanings of s.o.b. are:

> **SILLY OLD BUGGER**

> **SILLY OLD BASTARD**

Door bitch

Woman at the door of a club who decides who can enter and who can't. Also known as a 'door whore' because the two words rhyme ('dawr hawr').

Gay/homosexual (male)

There are many vulgar words for homosexuals which are generally used as insults.

Key words

Arse/bum bandit	*Batty boy*	*Fag*
Faggot	*Fruit*	*Homo*
Nancy boy	*Pansy*	*Poof*
Poofter	*Queer*	*Woofter*

I LIKE GEORGE - BUT HE'S A BIT OF A FRUIT

I HATE PANSIES, FAGS AND POOFTERS

BE CAREFUL IF YOU FIND YOURSELF ALONE WITH LENNY. HE'S A BIT OF A BUM BANDIT

Fag

Apart from meaning homosexual, fag can also mean cigarette - or it can mean 'tiresome'. It can also be used in some phrases as a euphemism for 'fuck'.

HE LIT HIS FAG WITH A LIGHTER

IT'S A FAG HAVING TO GET UP SO EARLY IN THE MORNING

I'M NOT A FAG

I CAN'T BE FAGGED TO DO ANY MORE WORK

BASTARD

Literally a bastard is the illegitimate child of unmarried parents. Apparently this is a word that is not used much in prisons because a great many of the people in prison really are illegitimate and it makes them very angry. It is rarely used with this literal meaning. It is usually just a general insult aimed at a man. The female version would be 'bitch'.

> **YOU NO GOOD BASTARD. WHY DID YOU LIE TO ME?**

> **YOU'RE A BASTARD!**

> **JOHN CAN BE A RIGHT BASTARD SOMETIMES BUT GENERALLY HE'S OK**

It was a bastard

It was very hard to do.

> **IT WAS A BASTARD TO GET THE TWO HORSES INTO THE HORSEBOX**

The bastard...

Used as an intensifier to express strong negative emotion – usually about a machine that isn't working properly. This is stronger than 'bloody' but not as strong as 'fucking'.

> **THE BASTARD CAR WOULDN'T START THIS MORNING**

> **THE BASTARD COMPUTER KEEPS CRASHING. I DON'T KNOW WHAT THE PROBLEM IS**

What a bastard!

A phrase of general sympathy on hearing a bad luck story.

> I LOST ALL MY MONEY IN THE STOCK MARKET CRASH...

> WHAT A BASTARD!

Fighting Talk

If someone says one of the phrases below then it is time to go. These are signals that the fighting might soon begin.

> DO YOU WANT TO MAKE SOMETHING OF IT?

> YOU'RE CRUISING FOR A BRUISING

> DO YOU WANT TO BE ON THE RECEIVING END OF A KNUCKLE SANDWICH?

> YOU WANT TO WATCH IT, MATE!

> IF YOU'RE NOT CAREFUL, I'M GOING TO FUCKING DO YOU

KNUCKLE SANDWICH

Sign Language

There are two common hand gestures that indicate anger.

The American hand sign
uses the middle finger.

The British tend to use
a two fingered signal

This is called the V sign – exactly the same name as the sign that Churchill made famous – and which Japanese teenagers like to make. The difference is that the happy V sign shows the palm of the hand towards the other person while the angry V sign shows the back of the hand to the other person.

To give someone the finger / V sign

'to give someone the finger' is to make a rude finger sign at them.

> I WAS SO ANGRY I GAVE HIM THE FINGER

> I GAVE HIM THE V SIGN

Miscellaneous insults

Airhead
Fool, idiot, dreamer – someone who is semi-permanently high on marijuana.

Cheapskate
A mean person.

DON'T BE A CHEAPSKATE

Chinless wonder
An unintelligent and rather useless member of the upper classes. A similar insult is 'hooray Henry', someone who is rich, uncaring and only interested in having a good time.

HE'S A CHINLESS WONDER

Creep
Unpleasant person, often weak and physically repugnant – or someone who acts in a disgusting way.

MY NEIGHBOUR IS A REAL CREEP

Deadbeat
A failure, loser, idle person.

DON'T SPEND ANY TIME WITH HIM.
HE'S JUST A DEADBEAT

Dodgy
Adjective describing someone or something that is not honest or can't be trusted.

JOHN'S BROTHER IS A BIT DODGY

Flake

A person who has odd ideas and/or cannot be depended on - adjective is flaky. (Also spelled flakey).

> **DON'T DEPEND ON JOHN. HE CAN BE VERY FLAKY**

Fuddy duddy

Affectionate term for an old fashioned person.

> **MY HUSBAND IS A BIT OF AN OLD FUDDY DUDDY**

Git

Annoying and contemptible person.

> **STUPID GIT!**

> **HE'S A MISERABLE OLD GIT**

Naff

Adjective meaning uncool, unfashionable, silly looking.

> **YOUR HAIRCUT IS TOTALLY NAFF**

Nutter

A crazy person.

> **STAY AWAY FROM HIM. HE'S A BIT OF A NUTTER**

Prat

A fool.

> **JOHN CAN BE A REAL PRAT SOMETIMES**

Prune

An unpleasant disapproving person and/or fool.

> **MY NEIGHBOUR IS A BIT OF A PRUNE**

Runt

Despicable smaller and weaker person – often used about children with whom one is angry. Adjectives: runty, runtish.

> YOU LITTLE RUNT!

> HE'S A RUNTY LITTLE MAN

Scaredy cat

Coward, easily frightened person.

> JOHN CAN BE A REAL SCAREDY CAT SOMETIMES

Sissy

Weakling, coward.

> DON'T BE A SISSY!

Slob

Disgustingly messy, often uncultured, badly dressed person.

> YOU CAN'T GO TO THE PARTY LOOKING LIKE A SLOB!

Smarmy

Adjective meaning to be nice in an oily way.

> I HATE PEOPLE WHO TRY TO BE SMARMY

Snot-nosed / Snotty / Snooty

Adjective meaning arrogant and snobbish.

> HE'S A SNOT-NOSED BASTARD

> DON'T BE SO SNOOTY!

Sourpuss

A sour-faced person, someone who grumbles a lot.

> JOHN IS A REAL SOURPUSS. HE
> NEVER SEEMS TO HAVE FUN

Time waster

Someone who isn't worth spending time with.

> DON'T PAY ANY ATTENTION TO HIM.
> HE'S JUST A TIME WASTER

Weedy

Weak and unassertive – especially physically.

> DON'T BE SO WEEDY!

Wimp

Weak and unassertive person – ineffectual and cowardly.

> I CAN BE A TERRIBLE WIMP
> SOMETIMES

Wuss

Weakling, someone who cannot be depended on. The adjective is wussy, meaning feeble or indecisive.

> DON'T BE SO WUSSY!

Yob/ Yobbo

Unthinking, aggressive, destructive male.

> THERE WERE SOME YOBS COMING
> TOWARDS ME SO I CROSSED THE ROAD TO GET
> OUT OF THEIR WAY

LANGUAGE OF THE LAVATORY___

SHIT

This is probably the second most commonly used vulgarity in English. The proper word for shit is 'excrement' or 'faeces' or, if we're talking about farming, then 'manure' is the word. Doctors who want to test it will ask you to provide some 'stool' for a 'stool test'. The proper verb is 'to defecate'.

Here are some examples of the literal use of shit:

> THERE'S A PIECE OF DOG SHIT ON THE FLOOR

> HE'S IN THE BATHROOM HAVING A SHIT

But there are many other idiomatic uses of the word.

Key words

Exclamations:

Shit!, shit a brick, eat shit!, no shit!, holy shit, tough shit!

Nouns:

Shit, a shit, a little shit, a shit stirrer, jack shit.

Verb forms:

*To be scared shitless, to beat the shit out of someone,
to drive someone apeshit (to go apeshit),
to drop someone in the shit, to eat shit,
to get one's shit together, to give someone shit,
to have the shit kicked out of (one), to have the shits,
to hit shit, to put the shit up someone,
to scare the shit out of someone, to shit bricks, to shit
someone, shit one's pants, to shit oneself, to take shit,
to talk shit, to treat someone like shit.*

Adjectives:

Shit, shitting awful, shitty, shitbox, chickenshit.

Phrases:

*Built like a brick shit house, full of shit,
happy as a pig in shit, in deep shit (in a whole lot of shit /
up shit creek / in shit street), not worth shit, same old shit,
shit for brains, shit happens, shit hot, shit scared,
shit in one's own backyard, shit loads, sure as shit,
when the shit hits the fan.*

Exclamations:

Shit! Oh Shit!

Here it is an exclamation used when something bad has happened or is about to happen or perhaps the speaker has got some bad news. In this meaning it is almost exactly the same as 'Oh God!', 'Oh Fuck!' and 'Damn!'. It is less acceptable than 'God' or 'Damn' but not as bad as 'fuck'.

OH SHIT! I'VE SPILT MY COFFEE

SHIT! WHAT DO I DO NOW?

OH SHIT! WHERE DID I PUT MY GLASSES?

Shit

This word can often be used as a kind of verbal pause, without any special meaning.

WELL, SHIT, I DON'T KNOW THE ANSWER

I DIDN'T KNOW WHAT TO DO SO, SHIT, I JUST WENT HOME

Shit a brick!

This is an exclamation of great surprise.

LOOK WHO'S HERE!...

WELL, SHIT A BRICK, ITS KEN. LONG TIME NO SEE!

Shit

The original old English word was the verb to shite which came from old German. The noun form, a shit, only appeared in the 16th century.

Eat shit!

This is an aggressively dismissive challenge meaning I don't care what you think.

> *I DON'T THINK YOU SHOULD DO THAT...*

> *WELL EAT SHIT! I DON'T CARE WHAT YOU THINK*

No shit!

This is a response that suggests surprise but is often used ironically, i.e. the speaker is not at all surprised. It can be used for both positive and negative surprise.

> *JOHN FAILED THE TEST...*

> *NO SHIT! WHAT A SURPRISE! MAYBE NEXT TIME HE'LL DO SOME WORK*

> *SAM AND TINA HAVE JUST GOT ENGAGED TO BE MARRIED...*

> *NO SHIT!*

Holy shit!

This is an expression of horror, or extreme surprise - you can also say 'holy fuck' but this is less common.

Tough shit!

This is an expression that means 'I don't care' or 'I completely lack any sympathy with you'.

Noun forms

Shit

Used as a noun, 'shit' can have the meaning of 'mess' or 'messy, dirty stuff' or 'dirty situation'.

> THE HOUSE WAS A MESS. THERE WAS
> A LOT OF SHIT ALL OVER THE PLACE

> THERE ARE PROBLEMS AT ANOTHER
> OFFICE AND I HAVE TO GO AND CLEAR
> UP THE SHIT

> DON'T GIVE ME ANY SHIT, OK?

Shit can also mean nonsense.

> WHAT YOU'RE SAYING IS A
> LOAD OF SHIT

Shit can also be used in a more general and abstract way – a vulgar variation on 'stuff'.

> HE DID HIS SHIT AND
> THEN WENT HOME

> YOU DO YOUR SHIT AND I'LL
> DO MINE

In this sense it often appears in the phrase '*...and shit like that*' meaning etcetera, and so on.

> HE BOUGHT SOME SHIRTS AND
> SOCKS AND SHIT LIKE THAT

> HE TALKED ABOUT BANKING AND
> INSURANCE AND SHIT LIKE THAT

Shit can also refer to any kind of drug.

I NEED SOME SHIT. WHAT HAVE YOU GOT?

I SMOKED SOME GOOD SHIT!

A shit!

This is one of those ways of saying you don't like a person, you think they are a bad person who does bad things. We can add words like '...head' or '...bag' or '...face' or '...arse' to add force to the word.

HE'S NOT REALLY A SHIT. HE'S JUST BEING A SHIT RIGHT NOW

NO. HE'S A TOTAL SHITHEAD

HE'S A COMPLETE SHITBAG

Little shit

This phrase is used to express anger at young children who have done something bad.

Jack shit

Aggressive way of saying 'nothing'.

> THE LITTLE SHIT THREW A STONE AT ME AND THEN RAN AWAY

> THE LITTLE SHIT STARTED SCREAMING

> A COUPLE OF LITTLE SHITS TRIED TO STEAL MY WALLET

A shit stirrer

A shit stirrer is someone who enjoys making problems worse or not letting a problem be forgotten.

> I'M GOING TO TELL JOHN WHAT MARY SAID ABOUT HIM...

> DON'T BE A SHIT STIRRER!

A shithole/shithouse

This can mean either a lavatory or a dirty disgusting place.

> WHERE'S THE SHITHOLE?

> HIS ROOM IS A SHITHOLE. REALLY, A COMPLETE SHITHOUSE

Verb phrases

Beat the shit out of someone (also: kick the shit...)

This phrase literally refers to a physical attack in which someone gets badly hurt.

> THEY BEAT THE SHIT OUT OF ME. I'M LUCKY TO BE ALIVE

Drive someone apeshit / go apeshit over something

This means to annoy someone to the point of craziness. To go crazy or to lose one's temper violently.

> THE WAY SHE BEHAVED DROVE ME COMPLETELY APESHIT

> SHE WENT COMPLETELY APESHIT WHEN SHE SAW WHAT I WAS DOING

Drop someone in the shit

This means to put someone in a situation where he will be blamed for something, or where he will suffer badly in some way.

> JOHN DROPPED ME IN THE SHIT TODAY. HE TOLD THE BOSS WHAT I HAD SAID ABOUT HIM

Eat shit

This is used mainly to mean 'to accept humiliation'.

> I MADE HIM EAT SHIT BEFORE I ACCEPTED HIS APOLOGY

Feel like shit

To feel unwell.

> HE DRANK TOO MUCH LAST NIGHT. HE FEELS LIKE SHIT THIS MORNING

Get (one's) shit together

This means to get organized or it can also mean to be a very organized kind of person.

> YOU'D BETTER START GETTING YOUR SHIT TOGETHER. WE'RE GOING IN TEN MINUTES

> JOHN HAS REALLY GOT HIS SHIT TOGETHER. I THINK HE'S GOING TO BE VERY SUCCESSFUL

Give someone shit

'Shit', in this phrase, can mean problems or excuses or negative information or interference.

> I CAN'T DO THE JOB...

> DON'T GIVE ME THAT SHIT! I KNOW YOU CAN DO IT

> HE TRIED TO GIVE ME SOME SHIT ABOUT HOW HE COULDN'T HELP ME, BUT I SORTED HIM OUT. HE'LL HELP US

Have the shit kicked out of you

This phrase can be used literally – someone attacked you and beat you up – or metaphorically – to have a lot of bad experiences which make you learn the hard way.

> I GOT INTO A FIGHT AND HAD THE SHIT KICKED OUT OF ME

> MY FIRST TWO YEARS IN THE JOB WERE VERY HARD. I HAD A LOT OF SHIT KICKED OUT OF ME

Have the shits

This literally means to have diarrhoea.

> I ATE SOMETHING BAD AND HAD A BAD CASE OF THE SHITS FOR A FEW DAYS

> I'VE HAD THE SHITS FOR THREE DAYS NOW

Hit shit

'To hit some shit' is to encounter some problems.

> THE NEGOTIATIONS WERE GOING FINE UNTIL WE HIT SOME SHIT OVER THE TERMS OF PAYMENT

Put the shit up (someone)

To be given a bad fright. This is the vulgar way of saying 'to put the wind up someone'.

> HE REALLY PUT THE SHIT UP ME. I THOUGHT I WAS GOING TO LOSE MY JOB

> I THOUGHT I WAS GOING TO BE KILLED. IT REALLY PUT THE SHIT UP ME

Be scared shitless

This is just one of the phrases connecting shit and fear. Some say that fear causes a desire to shit (be shit scared) and others suggest that fear causes an inability to shit (as here).

> I THOUGHT I SAW A GHOST. I WAS SCARED SHITLESS!

Scare the shit out of someone

This means to frighten someone.

> I DIDN'T HEAR HIM COME UP BEHIND ME. HE REALLY SCARED THE SHIT OUT OF ME

> LET'S TELL HIM THE BOSS IS ANGRY WITH HIM. THAT'LL SCARE THE SHIT OUT OF HIM

The adjective form of this phrase is 'to be shit scared'.

> THESE THREE BIG DOGS CAME RUNNING TOWARDS ME. I WAS SHIT SCARED

> I THREATENED TO PUNCH HIM. I CAN TELL YOU, HE WAS SHIT SCARED

Shit bricks

This means to be very frightened.

> I THOUGH I HEARD A GHOST. GOD I WAS SCARED. I WAS SHITTING BRICKS

Shit someone

This means to try to deceive or cheat someone.

> DON'T TRY AND SHIT ME

> YOU'RE SHITTING ME AND I DON'T LIKE IT

Shit on someone

To abuse or humiliate someone.

Shit (one's) pants

This phrase refers to the feeling of being very frightened.

Take shit

In this phrase, shit means abuse. If you 'take shit from somebody', this means they give you a lot of abuse.

> *IN MY LAST JOB I HAD TO TAKE A LOT OF SHIT FROM MY BOSS*

> *I DON'T TAKE ANY SHIT FROM ANYBODY*

Talk shit

This means to talk nonsense.

> *STOP TALKING SHIT*

Treat someone like shit!

This means to treat someone with no respect at all.

> *MY BOSS TREATS ME LIKE SHIT! ONE DAY I'M GOING TO DO SOMETHING ABOUT IT*

Adjectives

Shit/ shit at doing something

Used as an adjective it means bad or useless.

> *HE'S A SHIT DOCTOR*

> *I'M REALLY SHIT AT LYING. I JUST CAN'T DO IT*

Shitting awful

'Shitting' is used as an intensifier to make the word 'awful' more forceful.

> *I HAD A SHITTING AWFUL DAY*

> *IT WAS A SHITTING AWFUL MOVIE*

Shitty...!

This adjective means bad, nasty, objectionable.

I'VE GOT A SHITTY JOB

THAT WAS A SHITTY THING TO DO

Shitbox

Same as 'shitty' – applied to places.

IT WAS A SHITBOX MOTEL

Chickenshit

When said of a person it means cowardly or weak. In other contexts it can mean disgusting or inadequate or low quality. It can also be used as a noun.

IT WAS A CHICKENSHIT MOVIE

HE'S CHICKENSHIT. HE WON'T STAND UP TO YOU

DON'T BE SUCH A CHICKENSHIT

Phrases

Built like a brick shit house

This phrase is a disrespectful but admiring description of a large woman with large breasts, or a very big, strong man.

HE WAS BUILT LIKE A BRICK SHIT HOUSE

Full of shit

If a person is full of shit this means they should not be given any respect and should not be taken seriously.

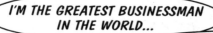

> I'M THE GREATEST BUSINESSMAN IN THE WORLD...

> YOU'RE JUST SO FULL OF SHIT!

> JOHN IS FULL OF SHIT! YOU CAN'T BELIEVE ANYTHING HE SAYS

Happy as a pig in shit

This is a phrase describing an extreme level of happiness.

> HIS WIFE GOES OUT TO WORK AND EARNS THE MONEY. HE'S GOT A MAID WHO DOES THE HOUSEKEEPING. HE'S HAPPY AS A PIG IN SHIT

> WANT TO JOIN ME?

Don't know shit from shinola

This is an American phrase meaning someone doesn't know anything. Shinola was a brand name for a brown shoe polish.

In deep shit / up shit creek (without a paddle) / in shit street / in a whole lot of shit

These phrases all mean to be in big trouble.

> I'M IN DEEP SHIT. MY WIFE FOUND OUT ABOUT THE GIRLFRIEND...

> YES, YOU'RE IN SHIT STREET, ALL RIGHT

> I HAVEN'T GOT ANY MONEY AND I'VE GOT NO JOB. I'M REALLY UP SHIT CREEK WITHOUT A PADDLE...

> YES, YOU'RE IN A WHOLE LOT OF SHIT, MY FRIEND

Not worth shit

This means: not worth anything.

> THIS PAINTING IS A FAKE. IT ISN'T WORTH SHIT!

On (one's) shit list

The vulgar version of 'to be in (someone's) bad books' meaning to be unpopular with someone.

> HE'S ON MY SHIT LIST

> I WOULD BE VERY SURPRISED IF I WASN'T ON HIS SHIT LIST

Same old shit

This phrase refers to things that don't change.

> HI JOHN. WHAT'S NEW?

> NOTHING. IT'S JUST THE SAME OLD SHIT

> I THOUGHT, WHEN WE GOT THE NEW BOSS, THAT THINGS WOULD CHANGE BUT NOTHING HAS CHANGED. IT'S JUST THE SAME OLD SHIT AS BEFORE

Shit all

This is the same as 'fuck all', meaning nothing.

> I'VE GOT SHIT ALL TO DO

> THERE'S SHIT ALL TO EAT IN THE FRIDGE

Shit for brains

This is an insult meaning 'stupid'.

> I DON'T KNOW HOW HE GOT HIS JOB. HE'S GOT SHIT FOR BRAINS

Shit happens.

This is a philosophical statement of acceptance. It means you can't avoid it, bad things happen. You have to accept that they happen and get on with life.

> I LOST MY JOB...

> AH WELL! SHIT HAPPENS

Shit hot

This phrase (surprisingly!) is a compliment meaning very good.

> WOW! THAT CAR IS SHIT HOT!

> LOOK AT THAT DANCER. SHE IS SHIT HOT!

Shit in one's own backyard

To do something that will only cause problems to oneself because it is very close to you.

> HE'S HAVING AN AFFAIR WITH HIS WIFE'S SISTER...

> THAT'S CRAZY. HE'S JUST SHITTING IN HIS OWN BACKYARD

> MY ADVICE TO YOU IS TO NEVER SHIT IN YOUR OWN BACK YARD

Shit loads

This means 'a lot'. Sometimes it is written as one word 'shitloads'.

> I'VE GOT SHIT LOADS OF WORK TO DO

Shit or get off the pot

This phrase means: do something (or make a decision), or if you can't do it, let someone else do it (make the decision).

> WELL, SHIT OR GET OFF THE POT

Sure as shit

This means: certainly, without any doubt.

> SURE AS SHIT IT WILL
> RAIN ON SUNDAY

> I THOUGH JOHN WOULD BE AT
> THE PARTY — AND, SURE AS SHIT,
> THERE HE WAS

When the shit hits the fan!

I don't know who invented this phrase but it is very graphic. Imagine a fan that is cooling the room. When the shit hits the fan it sprays all over the place. You can hide shit (i.e. problems, bad facts) but when shit hits the fan no-one can hide from it. This refers to a situation where a bad situation suddenly becomes very bad and explodes everywhere and has to be dealt with.

> WHEN THE SHIT HITS THE FAN, IT'S
> TIME TO DUCK DOWN AND WAIT TILL THE
> PROBLEM BLOWS OVER

Other Related Words
Key words and phrases

Bullshit	Bullshitter
To bullshit	A load of bull
Crap	Crappy
Be crap at	Beat the crap out of (someone)
Cut the crap	Dingleberry

Bullshit!

This means 'nonsense'. We say it when we disagree strongly with somebody or when we think someone is talking nonsense.

> **BILL CLINTON WAS THE BEST AMERICAN PRESIDENT THERE HAS EVER BEEN...**

> **BULLSHIT! HE WASN'T BAD BUT HE WASN'T GREAT**

A bullshitter

Someone who talks big or who tells lies.

> **YOU ARE SUCH A BULLSHITTER! YOU REALLY ARE!**

> **DON'T TRUST HIM. HE'S JUST A BULLSHITTER**

227

To bullshit

This means to trick or tease someone, to give them false information.

GUESS WHAT. YOU CAME TOP IN THE EXAM...

DON'T BULLSHIT ME!...

I'M NOT BULLSHITTING YOU. GO AND HAVE A LOOK YOURSELF

A load of bull

This means a lot of nonsense.

THE PRIME MINISTER GAVE US A LOAD OF BULL ABOUT WHAT A GOOD JOB HE WAS DOING FOR THE COUNTRY

CRAP

Crap is another word for shit. It carries a little less force, but only a little. It is still quite a bad word. But it has a different range of meanings.

Crap!

'Nonsense!'

LOS ANGELES IS REALLY A SAFE CITY...

THAT'S A LOAD OF CRAP

A crap (something)

Used as an adjective it means 'no good'.

> IT'S A CRAP CAR

> I'M A CRAP COOK

> THE FILM WAS ABSOLUTE CRAP

> THE PARTY WAS REALLY CRAP

Crappy

This means the same thing: i.e. no good.

> THE HOTEL WAS CRAPPY – BUT THE STAFF WERE FRIENDLY

> IT'S A CRAPPY BOOK BUT I COULDN'T STOP READING IT

Being crap at...

This phrase means 'I'm no good at (something)'.

> I'M CRAP AT TENNIS

> JOHN'S CRAP AT TELLING JOKES

> SUSAN IS CRAP AT TELLING LIES

Beat the crap out of someone

This means the same as 'beat the shit out of someone' and means to beat someone up quite badly.

> THE BULLIES ATTACKED THE SMALL BOY
> AND BEAT THE CRAP OUT OF HIM

Crap oneself

The same as 'to shit oneself' – to be very scared.

> BEFORE THE EXAM I WAS
> CRAPPING MYSELF

Cut the crap

This means 'stop talking nonsense'.

> CUT THE CRAP AND TELL ME WHAT
> REALLY HAPPENED

> HE STARTED TALKING ABOUT THE
> WEATHER SO I TOLD HIM TO CUT THE CRAP
> AND GET DOWN TO BUSINESS

Dingleberry

A small piece of shit that attaches itself to the hair round the anus. The rear ends of sheep tend to be full of dingleberries.

Euphemisms for shit:
Key words and phrases

Sugar!	*Shoot!*	*Sheesh!*

Sugar!
This is the euphemism for the exclamation 'Shit!'. Both words start with the same sound 'sh...'. It is quite common for a well brought up woman to say 'Oh Sugar!' when someone else might say 'Oh shit' – but that is the only use of shit that can be substituted by sugar. (We can't say: 'when the sugar hit the fan', or 'don't be a sugar' or 'she was sugar hot'.)

> OH SUGAR! MY MOBILE PHONE ISN'T WORKING!

Shoot!
Another euphemism is 'shoot'. This is typically American and almost polite. It is widely accepted. It can be used as an exclamation and as a meaningless word that marks a pause in the utterance.

> I'M FREE THIS EVENING...

> WELL, SHOOT. WHY DON'T WE GO OUT AND ENJOY OURSELVES?

> OH SHOOT! I'M GOING TO BE LATE AGAIN FOR WORK!

PISS

The fact that shit and piss are used so commonly explains why vulgar words in English are also referred to as 'dirty words'. Apart from urination, piss also refers to beer and its effects. In addition it is used in a number of vulgar idiomatic phrases.

Key words and phrases

> ### Piss (beer):
> Piss artist, pisshead, piss up, be pissed, pissed as a newt, out on the piss, gnat's piss.
>
> ---
>
> ### Other idiomatic phrases
> Piss about / around, piss all over someone, piss and moan, piss away, piss down, piss off, piss someone off, piss oneself / piss one's pants, take the piss out of someone, piece of piss, piss and vinegar, piss awful, pissed off, pissing, piss proud, piss-take, piss-taker.

Piss (beer)

One of the most important secondary meanings of piss is 'beer'. From this we get a couple of idiomatic uses.

A piss artist, a pisshead

This means either a person who is drunk now or a person who regularly gets drunk.

WHO'S THE PISSHEAD?

DON'T TAKE ANY NOTICE OF HIM. HE'S JUST A PISS ARTIST

A piss up

This is a party where a lot of drinking is done: usually a celebration.

> AFTER THE WEDDING WE HAD A BLOODY GREAT BIG PISS UP

> I'M PLANNING TO HAVE A PISS UP WHEN THE EXAM RESULTS COME OUT

To be pissed

In America this means to be angry (see 'be pissed off') but in British English it means to be drunk.

> I GOT PISSED LAST NIGHT

> I NEVER GET PISSED. AS SOON AS I FEEL THE SLIGHTEST BIT DRUNK I STOP DRINKING

To be pissed as a newt.

This means to be totally and completely drunk.

> I WAS PISSED AS A NEWT LAST NIGHT!

To be out on the piss

This phrase means to go out usually to a number of pubs and bars and have a good time drinking with friends.

> WHERE WERE YOU LAST NIGHT?...

> I WAS OUT ON THE PISS WITH JIM AND ALAN

Gnat's piss
Tasteless beer.

Other idiomatic phrases
Verb phrases
Piss about / piss around
This means to be silly, or not serious: to be foolish.

> IN MY SECOND YEAR AT UNIVERSITY
> I STOPPED PISSING ABOUT AND STARTED
> TO STUDY SERIOUSLY

> DON'T PISS ABOUT. BE SERIOUS!

Piss all over (someone) (also: to piss on (someone))
To be contemptuous of someone.

> HE SPENT THE WHOLE TIME
> PISSING ALL OVER ME

> I WANTED TO PISS ON HIM
> BUT I RESTRAINED MYSELF

Piss and moan
This means to complain continuously about something.

> STOP PISSING AND MOANING,
> WILL YOU? THERE'S NOTHING YOU CAN
> DO ABOUT IT!

> I'M FED UP WITH HIM. HE'S
> BEEN PISSING AND MOANING ALL
> MORNING

To piss away (something)

This means to waste, to squander something.

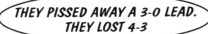

THEY PISSED AWAY A 3-0 LEAD.
THEY LOST 4-3

HIS FATHER LEFT HIM A LOT OF
MONEY BUT HE PISSED IT AWAY AND
NOW HE'S BROKE

To piss down

This is another way of saying it is raining hard.

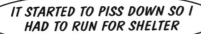

IT STARTED TO PISS DOWN SO I
HAD TO RUN FOR SHELTER

YOU'LL NEED AN UMBRELLA.
IT IS PISSING DOWN

Piss off

To piss off is to leave, go away, usually with the idea of doing it quickly.

THE POLICE CAME AND
EVERYONE PISSED OFF

WHY DON'T YOU PISS
OFF?

Piss

Piss came to England with the Norman invasion of 1066 from France. Related words can be found in old French pisser, Italian pisciare and German / Dutch pissen.

235

Piss (somebody) off

This means 'to make (someone) angry'.

> THE WAY SHE TALKS REALLY PISSES ME OFF

> IT PISSES ME OFF THAT THERE ARE SO MANY PEOPLE BEGGING IN THE STREETS

Piss oneself, to piss one's pants

This phrase is used to describe intense laughter, the idea is that you laugh so much you can't control yourself.

> I WAS LAUGHING SO MUCH I NEARLY PISSED MY PANTS

> I PISSED MYSELF LAUGHING SO MUCH

Take the piss (out of someone)

This means to make fun of someone, often by imitating them.

> I GET REALLY ANGRY WHEN PEOPLE TRY TO TAKE THE PISS OUT OF ME

> I ENJOY TAKING THE PISS OUT OF HIM. HE'S SO SERIOUS!

Extract the urine

a deliberately pompous way of saying 'take the piss' i.e. make fun of someone.

> ARE YOU TRYING TO EXTRACT THE URINE?

Miscellaneous

Piece of piss

This phrase means something is extremely easy to do. The polite version is 'a piece of cake'.

> **DID YOU HAVE ANY TROUBLE REPAIRING THE CAR?...**

> **NO. IT WAS A PIECE OF PISS**

Piss and vinegar

This means energy and enthusiasm.

> **I REALLY LIKE HIM. HE'S GOT THE RIGHT ATTITUDE – ALL PISS AND VINEGAR**

Piss awful

This word is used to describe a negative experience.

> **DID YOU ENJOY THE PARTY?...**

> **NO, IT WAS PISS AWFUL**

Pissed off

This is the British English adjective phrase meaning to be very angry about something.

> **I'M REALLY PISSED OFF THAT SHE DIDN'T INVITE ME TO THE PARTY**

> **JOHN WAS REALLY PISSED OFF WHEN WE PLAYED THAT TRICK ON HIM**

Americans use the phrase 'to be pissed' to express the same meaning.

> *I WAS REALLY PISSED THAT HE GOT THE JOB INSTEAD OF ME*

Pissing

We can use 'pissing' to add emphasis in the same way as 'fucking'.

> *IT WAS A PISSING AWFUL DAY*

> *WHERE'S THAT PISSING WAITER?*

> *WHAT'S THE PISSING TIME?*

Piss proud

This refers to a man's early morning erection.

> *HE WAS PISS PROUD*

Piss-take

A joke, making fun of someone.

> *IT WAS A PISS-TAKE*

Piss-taker

Someone who likes to take the piss out of other people.

> *DON'T MIND HIM. HE'S JUST A PISS-TAKER*

Piddling

Of very low importance

> *I'M NOT INTERESTED IN YOUR PIDDLING LITTLE PROBLEMS*

Other ways of saying 'Shit'

Formal/proper words:
To defecate, to evacuate the bowels,
to have a bowel movement.

Nice versions:
Do one's business, do a big job, do a biggie, do a number 2,
do a poo, do a poo-poo.

Vulgar versions:
To curl one off, to drop a load, to get a load off,
to have a crap, to have a dump, to have a shit,
to heave a Havana, to kak it, to lay a log, to poop one off.

Animal Excrement:
Cowpat, dung, manure, doo-doo,
dog poo, mess, poop, turds, droppings.

Ways of referring to diarrhoea and upset tummies

The runs, the squits, the trots, Montezuma's revenge,
Delhi Belly, the Mexican two step.

> **I'VE GOT A BAD CASE OF THE RUNS**

> **HE'S GOT DELHI BELLY OR MONTEZUMA'S REVENGE OR WHATEVER YOU WANT TO CALL IT**

Turd

This word that has ancient origins and, like 'shit,' originally referred to something that separated from the body.

Other ways of saying 'Piss'

Proper/formal words:
To urinate.

Nice phrases:
To empty one's bladder, to answer a call of nature,
to pass water, to have a tinkle, to have a wee-wee,
to have a wee.

Slightly vulgar phrases:
Have a leak, have a pee, have a widdle, have a piddle,
point percy at the porcelain,
shake hands with my wife's best friend.

More vulgar phrases:
Have a piss, have a slash.

Language for children

To urinate
To do number one, to have a pee, to have a wee wee.

To defecate
To do a poo, to do number two, to have a poo poo,
to do a big job, To do a ka-ka

Words for the lavatory

Proper/formal words:
The toilet, the lavatory, the W.C.*, the latrine(s)**,
the ladies', the gent's, the powder room, the facilities,
comfort station (U.S.).

Nice phrases:
The loo, the bathroom, the head(s)***, the can.

Vulgar phrases:
The jakes, the john, the bog(s), the pisshole, the shithole,
the crapper.

*stands for 'water closet'   **military   ***used on ships

How to say: I'm going to the toilet

Nice euphemisms for women
I need to powder my nose.
I'm just going to the little girl's room.
I just need to freshen up.
I need to spend a penny.

Nice euphemisms for men
I've got to see a man about a dog.
I think I'll go and inspect the plumbing.
I need to make a pit stop.
I'll just go and wash my hands.

Other toilet-related vocabulary

Bog roll: toilet paper
Bumf: toilet paper (short for bum fodder)
Floater: a turd that refuses to be flushed down
Throne, the: toilet bowl
Caught short: sudden, unexpected, need to use a toilet

Great stinking farts!

The polite way of referring to a fart is to say 'to break wind'.

More vulgar:

To blow off, to crack one off, to let one off

Strong smelling farts	**Loud farts**
A stinker,	To let rip,
A blind fart,	To let off a rip snorter,
An s.b.d (Silent but deadly)	To crack off a rasper

Phrases with 'fart'

Fart about/around

To mess around, to do something in an un-serious – or jokey – way.

> STOP FARTING AROUND AND
> GET BACK TO WORK

> WE DIDN'T DO MUCH WORK. WE SPENT
> THE WHOLE AFTERNOON FARTING AROUND

Fart along

To move slowly.

> WE FARTED ALONG AT ABOUT 50 KPH

Fart off

Hide from work.

> I DIDN'T GO BACK TO THE OFFICE. I
> JUST FARTED OFF ALL AFTERNOON

A brainfart
An idiotic idea.

Fartarse
a general insult, an incompetent person.

> DON'T BE SUCH A FARTARSE!

> HE DID THE WORK IN SUCH A FARTARSE WAY THAT I HAD TO GET SOMEONE ELSE TO DO IT AGAIN

Arty-farty
Pretentious, pretending to be artistic or intellectual.

> I DON'T LIKE HIM. HE'S TOO ARTY-FARTY FOR MY TASTE

Old fart
Old person – someone who is out of touch.

> MY SON THINKS I'M JUST AN OLD FART - AND MAYBE HE'S RIGHT!

Raspberry, blow a
You blow a raspberry when you make a noise with your lips that sounds like a fart.

> THAT WASN'T A REAL FART. THAT WAS JOHN BLOWING A RASPBERRY

Being drunk or on drugs

Many of the words used to describe being drunk can also be used to describe the effects of drugs – but not all. Unless otherwise indicated below, the words can be used in both contexts. Those words that apply only to alcohol are marked (i)

Polite words:
Drunk:
Happy, merry, inebriated.

On drugs:
High (high as a kite).

Slang but not vulgar words:
Banjoed, blasted, blitzed, blotto, bombed, clobbered, crocked, destroyed, lubricated(i), out of it, pickled(i), plastered(i), sloshed(i), smashed, sozzled(i), stoned, trashed, wasted, wrecked.

Vulgar words:
Arse-holed, bladdered, bolloxed, fucked, off (one's) tits, pissed(i), ratarsed, rat faced, shit faced, wankered.

> HE WAS TOTALLY PISSED!

> JOHN GOT HIMSELF TOTALLY ARSE-HOLED

> I HAD ONE DRINK TOO MANY AND I WAS COMPLETELY SHIT FACED BY THE TIME I GOT HOME

> HE WAS TOTALLY OFF HIS TITS

Vomiting

Drunkenness tends to lead to vomiting.

Key words

Nice:
Be sick, throw up.

Vulgar:
Chunder, a technicolour yawn, heave one's guts up, barf, blow one's groceries, lose one's lunch, puke, air (one's) guts, spew, chuck up.

HE WAS SICK ALL OVER THE FLOOR

HE THREW UP SEVERAL TIMES

THERE WAS A TECHNICOLOUR YAWN ALL OVER THE PAVEMENT

I HAD A GOOD CHUNDER AND IMMEDIATELY FELT MUCH BETTER

SHE HEAVED HER GUTS UP ALL OVER THE FLOOR

HE BARFED A FEW TIMES AND THEN FELT BETTER

HE BLEW HIS GROCERIES

HE HAD A FEW DRINKS TOO MANY AND HE LOST HIS LUNCH

SEX SLANG

In this chapter we list a variety of miscellaneous vulgar, slang and assorted sex-related vocabulary.

Mae West: *How tall are you young man?*

Man: *Six feet and seven inches.*

Mae West: *Well never mind about the six feet. Just give me the seven inches.*

Action
Whatever you are looking for: drugs, women, fun activity, the chance to do business.

> **WHERE'S THE ACTION?..**
>
> **ON SATURDAYS, MOST OF THE LATE NIGHT ACTION IS IN THE DANCE CLUBS**

Adult
Often used to refer to anything with strong sexual content. e.g. Adult publication, Adult entertainment.

Aroused
To become sexually excited.

Artist
Someone who has a particular ability. Some examples: backdoor artist (homosexual), piss artist (drunk), rip-off artist (cheat), wind-up artist (person who enjoys making other people angry), crap artist (liar).

> **DON'T DO BUSINESS WITH HIM. HE'S JUST A RIP-OFF ARTIST**

Babe
Girl. Sexually attractive female.

Babe magnet
A man that girls find attractive or an object like a sports car that is designed to attract the attention of 'babes'.

Baby, baby doll
Forms of address by a man to a girl/girlfriend (USA).

> *HEY BABY! HOW ARE YOU DOING?*

> *HEY BABY DOLL! YOU ARE LOOKING SO GOOD!*

Baby snatcher
Man who goes out with underage girl – or much younger woman.

Back breaker
Description of a woman who is athletically enthusiastic in bed.

> *DID YOU HAVE FUN LAST NIGHT?...*

> *YOU BET WE DID. SHE'S A REAL BACK BREAKER*

Banging shop
Brothel.

Barbie
A young attractive woman who is so perfectly dressed and made up that she looks like a Barbie doll.

BDSM
An abbreviation
of Bondage,
Domination,
Submission
and Manipulation.

> *HELLO. COULD I INTEREST YOU IN A LITTLE BDSM?*

Beau
Slightly old fashioned American word for boyfriend.

Bedroom antics
Newspaper slang for sexual activities.

Beefcake
Pictures of naked men.

Bestiality
Euphemism for sex with animals.

Bi
An abbreviation of 'bisexual' – someone who enjoys sex with both male and female partners – though not necessarily at the same time!

Bisexual
Other ways of saying the same thing:

Swing both ways

Ambidextrous
literally: can use both hands equally well – used in a jokey way

---

AC/DC
electrical terms meaning 'alternating current, direct current' – pronounced 'ai-see- dee-see')

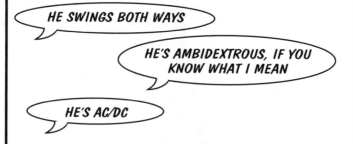

HE SWINGS BOTH WAYS

HE'S AMBIDEXTROUS, IF YOU KNOW WHAT I MEAN

HE'S AC/DC

Bi-curious
Someone who is interested in having a bisexual experience.

Bird
Girl.

Birds and bees
euphemism for sexual information.

> *I TOLD MY DAUGHTER ABOUT THE BIRDS AND BEES*

Bit
There are a number of phrases using 'bit' that can refer to:

(i) sex: bit of cunt, bit of cock, bit of tickle, bit of how's your father, bit of fun.

(ii) women: bit of skirt, bit of stuff.

Bit on the side
Either sexual intercourse outside one's main relationship – or the person (either sex) that provides it.

> *HE'S MARRIED BUT THAT DOESN'T STOP HIM GOING FOR A BIT ON THE SIDE WHEN HE HAS A CHANCE*

Blind date
To go out with someone who one hasn't met before.

> *I MET HER ON A BLIND DATE*

Bodacious
New American word for a woman with a very sexy body. A combination of body + audacious. Another similar word is bodelicious: body + delicious. Not current in Britain.

Bombshell
Same as sex bomb – a very sexy woman.

Bondage
Tying someone for the purpose of sexual excitement.

Boob job
Plastic surgery on the breasts.

Boob tube
An elasticated strapless top worn by young women.

Brewers droop
The inability to have an erection caused by drinking too much alcohol.

Brown shower
The use of shit as part of sexual activity.

Brown sugar
Sexy black girl or sex with black girl.

Brush off
To give someone the brush off is to make it very clear you are not interested in starting a relationship.

Buff, in the
Naked.

Being 'Naked'

Nice
*In the all together, in his/her birthday suit, in the buff,
in the nude, in the nudie, in the raw, completely starkers.*

Vulgar
Stark bullock naked, bare-assed.

Other words involving nakedness
To streak: *run naked in a public place*
Go skinny dipping: *to go swimming without any clothes on*
Get one's kit off: *to get undressed*

Bung hole
Anus, vagina – sometimes also mouth.

Busty
Having large breasts.

Butch
Describing a lesbian who is very masculine and aggressive.
Also *bull dyke, bull-bitch dyke* – an aggressively dominant
lesbian.

Call girl
High class prostitute.

Camp
An adjective describing men who act in an exaggeratedly effeminate way. Some people – typically some homosexuals - are like this much of the time.

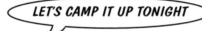

Camp it up
To act in an exaggeratedly effeminate way for fun.

Canoodle
To canoodle is to kiss and hug.

Carnal knowledge
Old fashioned formal phrase meaning sexual intercourse.

Casting couch
A sofa in a film director's office supposedly used for sex with attractive women who wish to get a part in a film.

Casual sex
Sex without obligations.

Caught with pants down
'To be caught with one's pants down' is to be caught unprepared in an embarrassing situation.

Charms
Used of a woman to refer to her breasts (or other sexual parts).

Chat up
Talk to a person of the other sex as the first stage of seduction.

> LET'S CHAT UP THESE GIRLS

Cheap
To have a bad reputation for being sexually easy. To feel sexually dirty.

> I DON'T WANT PEOPLE TO THINK
> I'M CHEAP

> I FEEL CHEAP EVERY TIME HE
> LOOKS AT ME LIKE THAT

Cheat on
'To cheat on someone' is to have a sexual relationship outside marriage or steady relationship.

> SHE'S CHEATING ON HER BOYFRIEND

Cheesecake
Pictures of naked women.

Cherry
a) a virgin's hymen. To lose one's cherry is to lose one's virginity.

b) a young attractive woman.

> SHE LOST HER CHERRY WHEN
> SHE WAS SIXTEEN

> SHE'S A REAL CHERRY

Chick
Girl.

Chicken-hawk
Older person who has a sexual interest in very young people.

Clap (also pox)
'To have the clap' or 'the pox' means to have a sexual disease.

Cleavage
The space between a woman's breasts.

HMM! NICE CLEAVAGE!

Clip joint
Cheap nightclub where you can expect to be cheated by the staff.

Closet, come out of
To reveal oneself publicly as a homosexual.

HE CAME OUT OF THE CLOSET A FEW YEARS AGO AND IS MUCH HAPPIER AS A RESULT

Closet queen
Homosexual who tries to keep his sexuality hidden – also 'closet fag'.

Cluster fuck
Gay slang for group sex session.

Cocksman
A virile womanizer.

Cock teaser
A woman who pretends she is interested in sex but in the end decides she isn't. (also: prick teaser).

> *I THOUGHT IT WAS MY LUCKY NIGHT BUT SHE TURNED OUT TO BE A COCK TEASER*

Cocky
Arrogant.

> *I'M THE GREATEST!...*

> *DON'T BE SO FUCKING COCKY!*

Coed
An American term for 'girl student' – deriving from co-education (i.e. the education of girls and boys together in the same class).

Colourful
Interesting in a rather naughty way.

> *JOHN HAS HAD A VERY COLOURFUL PAST*

Combine sex with travel
'To combine sex with travel' is a joking reference to the phrase 'fuck off'.

> *I THINK YOU SHOULD COMBINE SEX WITH TRAVEL...*

> *WHAT DO YOU MEAN?...*

> *I MEAN FUCK OFF! GO AWAY. GET OUT OF HERE!*

Cop off with
To have a sexual experience with someone.

> WHILE HIS WIFE WAS AWAY HE COPPED
> OFF WITH ONE OF HER FRIENDS

Cradle snatcher
Man who goes out with a much younger woman (see baby snatcher).

Cream one's pants
This phrase is used for men who find someone really very sexy – so sexy that they want to have an orgasm without doing anything.

> SHE WAS SO SEXY I NEARLY
> CREAMED MY PANTS

Cream someone
To cream someone is to defeat them or do something much better than another person, to win at something easily. This is a classic example of sexual language referring to forms of aggression.

> MANCHESTER UNITED GOT REALLY CREAMED
> YESTERDAY. THEY LOST 5-0

> WE CREAMED THE OPPOSITION

Cruise
To walk around looking for people to meet.

> WE CRUISED ALL THE BARS BUT
> THERE WASN'T ANY ACTION

Crush
'To have a crush on someone' means to fall in love with them from a distance.

I'VE GOT A REAL CRUSH ON MY HISTORY TEACHER!

Cunning linguist
Cunnilingus is the formal word for oral sex done to a woman. A joke play on words is 'cunning linguist' – meaning a man who enjoys cunnilingus.

Curse
A woman's monthly menses – also known as menstrual period – or just period, or 'that time of the month'.

I'M HAVING MY PERIOD

I'VE GOT THE CURSE

Cute
Attractive in a very young way.

Cutesy
Is to be overly cute in a contrived way.

Cybersex
Sexual contact mediated by a computer (see Virtual sex).

D

Date, to
As a verb it means to go out with a person of the opposite sex, generally it has a sense of meeting regularly.

SHE'S DATING THREE DIFFERENT MEN

Date, to go out on
This means to go out for an evening with a person of the
other sex that one finds attractive. Also 'to have a date'.

> I'VE GOT A DATE ON FRIDAY
> EVENING

> I'M GOING OUT ON A DATE
> ON FRIDAY

Date
As a noun it refers to the person that one his having a date
with. This usage is particularly American.

> SHE'S MY DATE FOR TONIGHT

Deflower
To break the hymen and so end a girl's state of virginity.

> SHE WAS DEFLOWERED WHEN SHE
> WAS 17 YEARS OLD

Dildo
An imitation penis used for sexual games or masturbation.

Dirty
Sexually disapproving.

> SHE THINKS ORAL SEX IS DIRTY

Dirty old man
Older man who acts in a lecherous way.

> *GET YOUR HANDS OFF ME, YOU*
> *DIRTY OLD MAN!*

Ditch
'To ditch someone' is to end the relationship.

> *SHE DITCHED ME FOR*
> *ANOTHER MAN*

Other expressions with the same meaning as 'to ditch someone'

Dump someone	*Give someone the boot*
Break up with someone	*Break it off with someone*
Split up with someone	
To give someone the kiss off	
Give someone the old heave ho	

> *SHE DUMPED ME*

> *SHE GAVE ME THE BOOT*

> *HE BROKE IT OFF WITH HER*

> *SHE SPLIT UP WITH HIM*

> *SHE GAVE HIM THE KISS OFF*

> *HE GAVE HER THE OLD HEAVE HO*

Dolly bird
Attractive girl or young woman usually dressed in the very latest fashions.

> LOOK AT THAT DOLLY BIRD!

Doggy-style
Used to describe the sex position where the man stands behind the woman who is bent forward.

Dominatrix
A woman who physically abuses men as a sex game. Also known as a dom.

Drag
If a man is 'in drag', he is dressed and made up as a woman. A drag can also mean a tiresome job or a fact of life.

> 'WHAT A DRAG IT IS GETTING OLD'

line from a Rolling Stones song.

> I HAVE TO GET UP AT 5.30 EVERY MORNING. IT'S A DRAG BUT I DON'T HAVE ANY CHOICE

> HE WAS IN DRAG SO I DIDN'T RECOGNIZE HIM

Drag queen
A man who enjoys dressing up as a woman.

Drool over someone
To look at someone or something with great sexual interest.

Dyke, lezzie
Lesbian/female homosexual.

E ——————

Earthy
Sexy in an open and direct way, also used of bad language.

> HE USED VERY EARTHY LANGUAGE

> SHE'S VERY SEXY IN AN EARTHY SORT OF WAY

Elevator eyes
A way of describing the look a man gives an attractive woman when he looks her 'up and down'.

> HE'S GOT ELEVATOR EYES

Erotica
Nice, approving word for sexually exciting writing or pictures. Some feminists have stated that erotica is what women like and pornography is what men like. Another way of describing the difference between erotica and pornography is this: "Erotica is when you use a feather. Pornography is when you use the whole chicken."

Escort
High class paid-for sex companion.

Ex-
Means previous (i.e. ex-husband, ex-girlfriend etc.) but on its own it means ex-husband or ex-wife.

> IT'S A STRANGE WORLD. MY EX IS NOW GOING OUT WITH MY SISTER'S EX

Exotic
Strange and unusual, from a distant country. Suggests dark skinned and sexy – also used as a tempting description at a strip club: 'exotic dancers'.

Explicit
The main meaning is: to show something very clearly. In many contexts it means that something shows a lot of nudity and sex.

> THE FILM WAS VERY EXPLICIT

Eye fuck
To look at someone with strong sexual interest.

> STOP EYE FUCKING THE WOMEN AND PAY ATTENTION TO ME

Eye up
To look at with sexual interest.

> THE GIRLS WERE EYEING UP THE BOYS AND VICE VERSA

F ——————

Facial
To give someone a facial is for a man to ejaculate semen on to his lover's face.

Facts of life
Sex information, information about the realities of life.

> MY DAD WAS TOO EMBARRASSED TO TELL ME THE FACTS OF LIFE

Fag hag
Female friend of a gay man.

Fake it
To pretend one has had an orgasm.

> *HALF THE TIME I FAKE IT, BUT MY*
> *BOYFRIEND DOESN'T KNOW THAT*

Fall for
To become sexually attracted.

> *HE'S REALLY FALLEN FOR HER*
> *IN A BIG WAY*

Fall in love
A total feeling of new love. Sometimes given extra emphasis by the phrase 'head over heels'.

> *I FELL HEAD OVER HEELS IN LOVE*
> *WITH MY FIRST BOY FRIEND*

Falsies
Bra pads that make a woman's bust look bigger.

Fancy
To fancy someone is to find him or her sexually attractive.

> *I REALLY FANCY HIM*

Fancy man
A pimp – also a young male lover of an older woman (see toy boy).

Fanny magnet
Anything that is likely to attract the interest of attractive women (a sports car etc.) – see babe magnet.

Fan one's pussy
Said of a woman who moves in a sexual way designed to get someone's attention.

LOOK AT HER FANNING HER PUSSY AT YOU. SHE IS SHAMELESS

Fast
(Old fashioned) a woman was said to be fast if she had an active sex life.

Fast food sex
Quick, spontaneous sex with a stranger.

Feel frisky
To feel like you want to have sex.

Feel up
To 'feel someone up' is to touch their sexual parts in order to excite them.

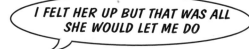

I FELT HER UP BUT THAT WAS ALL SHE WOULD LET ME DO

Felch
Gay slang for the act of licking semen from his lover's anus. A felcher is someone who enjoys doing this.

Fella
Boyfriend. May be spelled 'fellow' (the proper spelling) but is always pronounced 'fella' – and usually also written this way.

SUE'S GOT A NEW FELLA

Femme
The ultra feminine role in a lesbian relationship – to complement someone who is 'butch'.

> **MARY IS THE FEMME IN THAT RELATIONSHIP**

...fest
This is added on to the end of a word to suggest a party involving a lot of people having fun doing something: a fuckfest would be an orgy. *Fuckfest, bonkfest, shagfest, gropefest.*

Finger/fist
'To finger/fist a woman involves inserting that part of the hand up the vagina.

Fire blanks
This is what a man does after he has had a vasectomy. He ejaculates but he can't make a woman pregnant.

Flamboyant
The formal meaning is to be showy – but newspapers reserve the word as a euphemism for extrovert homosexuals.

> **HE LEADS A FLAMBOYANT EXISTENCE, IF YOU GET MY MEANING**

Flat chested
Description of a woman who has small breasts.

> **SHE'S REALLY GOOD LOOKING. THE ONLY PROBLEM IS THAT SHE'S A BIT FLAT CHESTED**

Flash

To flash is to expose oneself sexually in public. A 'Flasher' is someone who flashes.

> THERE'S AN OLD FLASHER WHO SOMETIMES STANDS OUTSIDE THE GIRLS' SCHOOL. HE FLASHES THEM WHEN THEY COME OUT. I WISH THE POLICE WOULD DO SOMETHING ABOUT HIM

Flesh market

Brothel, place people go to find sex partners.

Flex (one's) sex

Have an erection.

Fling

Casual affair, or short term sexual relationship.

> I HAD A FEW FLINGS WHILE I WAS AT UNIVERSITY BUT NOTHING SERIOUS

Flirt, to

To flirt is to play a playful game with people that you are sexually attracted to.

> I FLIRTED WITH HER ALL AFTERNOON. IT WAS GREAT FUN

Flirt, a
Someone who plays flirting games but refuses to continue to more serious sexual engagement. Not a good thing to be.

> **SHE'S JUST A FLIRT**

Flirtatious
To be the kind of person who enjoys flirting.

> **SHE ENJOYED BEING FLIRTATIOUS WITH ALL THE YOUNG MEN**

Flirty
A more modern way of saying flirtatious.

Fondle
To touch and stroke in a sexual way.

> **I LIKE IT WHEN MY LOVER HOLDS ME IN HIS ARMS AND FONDLES ME**

Forbidden fruit
Girl who is underage for sex.

Foreplay
Sexual activity as a warm up before full sexual intercourse.

> **HE'S NOT A GOOD LOVER. HE DOESN'T SPEND MUCH TIME ON FOREPLAY**

Foxy
Sexy.

French kiss
To kiss with tongue play.

> **I TRIED TO GIVE HER A FRENCH KISS BUT SHE PUSHED ME AWAY**

French letter
Condom.

Friar tuck
Australian rhyming slang for fuck.

I COULD DO WITH A FRIAR TUCK

Fridge
A frigid (ie sexually cold) woman – a woman who has no interest in sex.

Frolic
To play in a carefree way – can be a euphemism for a fun sexual experience.

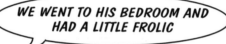

WE WENT TO HIS BEDROOM AND HAD A LITTLE FROLIC

Frottage
The rubbing of a man's genitals against a woman in a crowded place eg. rush-hour train. Man who does this is a frotteur. Verb: to frot.

Fuck pad
An apartment used mainly for sex.

Funny ideas
Ideas of doing something bad or wrong – usually of a sexual nature.

DON'T GET ANY FUNNY IDEAS!

Fuzz/Fuzzies
Pubic hair.

G spot
A spot of extreme pleasurable sensitivity in the female genital area.

> HE'S A WONDERFUL LOVER. HE ALWAYS MANAGES TO HIT MY G-SPOT

G-string
A minimal bikini bottom worn by dancers and strippers. (Also 'thong')

> THE DANCERS WORE G-STRINGS AND NOTHING ELSE

Game, be (go) on
'To go on the game' is to become a prostitute.

> DID YOU HEAR? PAULA IS ON THE GAME

Gangbang
A situation where several men rape one woman (occasionally not rape but consenting).

Gang rape
Rape by a group of men.

Gangsta
Sexually aggressive, possibly criminal, black man.

Gangsta bitch
Woman who associates with a gangsta.

Gay
Approving word meaning homosexual.

> HE FINALLY TOLD HIS PARENTS
> HE WAS GAY

Gender bender
A transvestite or transsexual.

Get it on with
To have sex with someone.

> I HEAR YOU GOT IT ON WITH
> LINDA LAST WEEK

Get it together
Start a sexual relationship.

> I LIKE YOU AND I THINK YOU LIKE ME
> SO WHY DON'T WE GET IT TOGETHER?

Get it up
Have an erection.

> I WAS SO NERVOUS I
> COULDN'T GET IT UP

Get off with
Manage to have sex with.

> I GOT OFF WITH A GIRL I MET
> AT THE CLUB

Get to first base
To put one's hand on a girl's breasts. The phrase comes from the sport of baseball.

Give (someone) the eye
To make eye contact with someone as a way of showing one's sexual interest.

> SHE GAVE ME THE EYE SO I WENT
> OVER TO TALK TO HER

Glory hole (1)
Vagina.

Glory hole (2)
Hole in a wall – in a toilet for example – for sticking one's penis through for anonymous homosexual encounters.

Go all the way
Have complete sex.

> SHE REFUSED TO GO ALL THE WAY

Go at it like rabbits
Have energetic sex.

Golden shower
Urination as a part of sexual activity.

Goose
When a man gooses a woman he puts his hand up her skirt and pinches or tickles her genital area. It also means to grab a man's testicles from behind as a joke.

> I WAS WALKING THROUGH A CROWD
> WHEN SOMEONE GOOSED ME

Gooseberry

A gooseberry is a third person who won't leave a couple who want to be alone together.

> *I WANTED TO BE ALONE WITH JOHN BUT MARY WAS THERE BEING A GOOSEBERRY*

Go out with

Be in a boy/girlfriend type of relationship with someone.

> *JOHN HAS BEEN GOING OUT WITH SALLY FOR SEVERAL YEARS NOW*

Go steady

Be in a boy/girlfriend type of relationship with someone. American.

> *WE'VE BEEN GOING STEADY FOR A FEW WEEKS NOW*

Gratuitous sex

Sexual scenes in a film that are not necessary to tell the story but which are included to attract people to see the film.

Grope

To meddle with someone's sexual parts with one's hands (also: 'to touch up', 'to feel up' and 'to cop a feel') – used both as a noun and as a verb.

> *THEY HAD A QUICK GROPE BEHIND THE TREE*

> *SHE GROPED HIM WHEN NO-ONE ELSE WAS LOOKING*

Groper
Someone who gets his kicks by touching women's breasts or buttocks.

THE TRAIN WAS VERY CROWDED. SHE FELT A GROPER'S HAND ON HER BUM BUT SHE COULDN'T SEE WHO WAS DOING IT

Gross
Disgusting.

YUK! THAT'S REALLY GROSS

Groupie
Young girl who follows rock stars and hopes to have sex with them.

H ———

Half mast
If a man is 'at half mast' he only has a partial erection.

Hand job
To bring someone to orgasm using the hand.

SHE GAVE HIM A HAND JOB

Hanky panky
Humorous way of referring to sexual activity.

JOHN AND MARY WERE CAUGHT HAVING A LITTLE HANKY PANKY IN THE BATHROOM

Hardcore porn
Pictures, videos etc of explicit sexual acts.

Have one's wicked way with...
Have sex with.

Have the horn for
For a man to feel sexually aroused by someone.

> I'VE REALLY GOT THE HORN FOR
> JOHN'S SISTER

Head-turner
A woman who is so attractive that men turn to look at her.

> YOUR MOTHER WAS A REAL HEAD-TURNER
> WHEN SHE WAS YOUNG

Heart throb
Person who makes people fall in love with them – usually public figures: pop stars, actors etc.

Heart to heart
To have an honest, intimate conversation.

> WE HAD A HEART TO HEART CONVERSATION
> ABOUT OUR FEELINGS FOR EACH OTHER

Hen party
A women-only party for the bride – often the night before the wedding (see: stag party).

Hickey
A bruise made deliberately by one's lover (see: love bite).

Hit on
To make sexual advances on someone.

> HE TRIED TO HIT ON ME BUT I
> WASN'T INTERESTED

Hit skin
Have sex (also 'bump bellies').

Homophobic
Hating homosexuals.

> THE TROUBLE WITH TIM IS THAT
> HE'S HOMOPHOBIC

Honey
A lovely girl or a nice helpful boy. A sweet way of calling your loved one. Also: honey bunch!

> COULD YOU BE A HONEY AND HELP ME
> CARRY THIS BOX? THANKS

> HI, HONEY, HOW WAS YOUR DAY?

Honey fuck
An underage girl who has sex.

Hooker
Prostitute.

Hop into bed with
To have casual sex with someone.

> I'D HOP INTO BED WITH HER ANYTIME

Horns
To give someone horns or to put the horns on someone: a wife does this to her husband if she has an affair with someone else. Old fashioned term.

Horny:
Feeling in need of sex.

> SHE'S A HORNY BITCH!

> GOD! I FEEL SO HORNY!

Hot
Sexy, exciting.

Hot date
Sexually exciting date.

Hot for (something)
Very interested in doing something – strong sexual overtones.

Hot item
Strongly romantic sexual relationship.

Hot number
Sexually attractive woman.

Hots
The phrase is 'to have the hots for someone'. This phrase means to be very attracted to someone sexually.

JOHN HAS THE HOTS FOR SUSAN

Hot to trot
Eager for sex.

House of ill repute
Brothel.

Hung
To have large genitals – usually in the phrase 'well hung'.

GEE! SHE IS SO CUTE AND INNOCENT

HOLY FUCK! I BET HE'S HUNG LIKE A GODDAMN HORSE

Hunk
Very handsome man.

Indecent
A disapproving euphemistic word relating to sex.

> THE WAY SHE DRESSES IS QUITE
> INDECENT. FAR TOO REVEALING

Indecent assault
A sexual assault – usually some form of touching – that is less than rape.

Infatuated
To be obsessed with the feeling of love for someone. The noun is infatuation.

> IT'S NOT REAL LOVE. IT'S JUST
> INFATUATION

> I WAS REALLY INFATUATED WITH
> MY HISTORY TEACHER

Intimate
To be very close to someone. We can describe close friends who share all their secrets as intimate friends. But the word also has a sexual sense – used as a formal, legal, euphemism for having sex.

> HE WAS INTIMATE WITH HER ON
> THREE OCCASIONS

Intimacy
This is the noun form of 'intimate'.

> HE WAS ALONE IN THE ROOM WITH HER FOR OVER AN HOUR BUT NO INTIMACY TOOK PLACE

In the saddle
To be in the act of having sex. To be the person on top during sexual intercourse.

> I LIKE IT WHEN THE WOMAN IS IN THE SADDLE

Item
A confirmed boy/girlfriend relationship.

> JOHN AND MARY ARE AN ITEM NOW

J ———

Jailbait
Girl who is underage for sex.

> DON'T TRY ANYTHING WITH HER. SHE'S JAILBAIT

Jig-a-jig
Sexual intercourse. A prostitute's invitation.

> YOU WANT TO JIG-A-JIG WITH ME?

Jock
Young athletic male.

Juice up
Get (someone) sexually excited. Can also mean to become drunk.

> *I WENT TO THE BAR AND GOT*
> *TOTALLY JUICED UP*

> *I JUICED HER UP NICE AND SLOWLY*

Juicy
Sexy.

Jump someone's bones
Have sex with someone (something a man might say).

Kept woman
A woman who is given regular money in exchange for a long term sexual relationship.

Kerb crawler
Man who drives slowly soliciting women for sex. The act is kerb crawling.

> *KERB CRAWLING IS NOW ILLEGAL*

Kinky
Sexually eccentric.

> *HE'S INTO A LOT OF KINKY SEX*
> *LIKE DRESSING UP IN UNIFORM AND*
> *SPANKING AND SO ON*

Kiss and tell
To talk about one's private life in public – especially to talk about one's sexual activities with famous people.

> I DON'T LIKE PEOPLE WHO KISS AND TELL.

Kit
Jokey way of referring to clothes.

> GET YOUR KIT OFF

Knee trembler
To have sex in a standing position against a wall.

> I WAS COMPLETELY DRUNK BUT I MANAGED TO HAVE A KNEE TREMBLER WITH SOMEONE I MET AT THE CLUB

Knickers
Female underpants.

Knickers!
An exclamation meaning: Nonsense! Rubbish!

Knickers in a twist
To be so anxious about something that you can't stop fussing.

> JOHN HAS GOT HIS KNICKERS IN A TWIST ABOUT THE OFFICE INSPECTION

> DON'T GET YOUR KNICKERS IN A TWIST!

Knocking shop
Brothel.

Knock off
To knock someone off is to have sex with them – often on a regular basis.

> THE MANAGER IS KNOCKING OFF HIS SECRETARY

L ———

Lad
Refers approvingly to young male who drinks a lot and has lots of girlfriends. Generally used in the phrase 'a bit of a lad'.

Lascivious
A slightly disapproving word meaning having too much interest in sex. Not as strong as lecherous (see below).

Lech
To find someone sexually attractive.

> I'VE GOT A BIG LECH FOR MY NEXT-DOOR NEIGHBOUR

Lecher
A man who is always looking at women as sexual objects. The noun form is lechery.

> I SUPPOSE I'M A BIT OF A LECHER BUT I SAY THERE'S NOTHING WRONG WITH A LITTLE LECHERY

Lecherous
Disapproving word for someone whose behaviour shows too much interest in sex.

> I DON'T LIKE HIM AT ALL. HE'S LECHEROUS

Leg man
A man who particularly likes to look at women's legs. Also 'ass man', 'tit man'.

Lewd
Disgusting in a sexual way.

> **MANY PEOPLE WILL CONSIDER THIS BOOK TO BE FULL OF LEWD WORDS**

Liberated
Not having inhibitions about sex.

Limp dick
(i) a penis that won't become erect or
(ii) an uninteresting person.

Loins
A word that refers to the genital area in a very imprecise way. It is commonly found in the Bible.

> **HE COVERED HIS LOINS**

Lonely hearts
Personal advertisements from people seeking to meet others for a relationship. They appear in a lonely hearts column or personals column.

Loose
Slightly dated critical comment on a woman who is considered to be sexually available.

> **PEOPLE WILL THINK YOU'RE A LOOSE WOMAN**

Love affair
A loving relationship.

> **WE HAD A BRIEF BUT INTENSE LOVE AFFAIR A FEW YEARS AGO AND WE HAVE REMAINED FRIENDS EVER SINCE**

Love birds
A couple who are showing they are in love.

Love bite
A bruise made by sucking a person's flesh.

Love button
Clitoris.

Love child
Child born outside marriage.

Love handles
Folds of fat flesh at the waist (also known as a spare tyre).

Lover
Person one has (or had) a sexual relationship with.

Lovey-dovey
Description of someone who is over-affectionate in a slightly actorish way.

> HE'S VERY LOVEY-DOVEY BUT YOU'LL LIKE HIM

Lust
'To be in lust with someone' or 'to lust after someone' is to find someone very attractive sexually.

Lusty
Full of sexual energy.

> SHE'S A LUSTY GIRL

M ——————

Macho
To be strongly and aggressively masculine. Pronounced 'match –o' but often mispronounced 'ma-ko'.

> THEY SAY SPANISH MEN ARE VERY MACHO. IS THAT TRUE?

Machismo
The culture of aggressive masculinity.

> MACHISMO IS ALIVE AND WELL IN SOUTH AMERICA

Maidenhead
A nice way of referring to the hymen.

Make advances
To show sexual interest in seducing someone. Also 'make a
play for' and 'make a pass at' (American)

> HE MADE ADVANCES ON HER
> AND SHE DIDN'T RESIST

> HE MADE A PLAY FOR HER

> HE MADE A PASS AT HER

Make, on the
To be on the look out for some easy sex.

> KEEP AWAY FROM HIM. HE'S
> ALWAYS ON THE MAKE

Make out
Kiss, cuddle, have sex.

> WE SPENT THE AFTERNOON
> MAKING OUT

Make, put on
'To put the make on (someone)' is to try to seduce them in a
slightly aggressive way.

Make-up sex
When a couple have a big argument and then make friends
again they may have passionate sex. This is referred to as
make-up sex.

Mate
As a noun it means 'friend' – often used as a friendly greeting to a stranger – and as a verb it means to have sexual intercourse for the purpose of producing children – usually used with breeding animals.

> HELLO, MATE! WHAT CAN I DO FOR YOU?

> I WENT OUT WITH MY MATES

> I WANT TO MATE MY MARE WITH YOUR STALLION

Menage à trois
A French phrase to express an arrangement in which three people live together in a sexual relationship.

Missionary position
The position in which missionaries supposedly have sex. The woman is on her back and the man is on top of her. No fancy stuff!

Mister Right
The right person for a woman.

> GUESS WHAT! I THINK I'VE FOUND MR. RIGHT

Mistress
Woman who is maintained by a man for sexual purposes.

> RICH MEN ARE EXPECTED TO HAVE ONE OR TWO MISTRESSES

Modesty
Shyness – especially in relation to sex or nudity.

> SHE USED A TOWEL TO
> PROTECT HER MODESTY

Moll
Girl, girlfriend (usually of a gangster) – old fashioned.

Mount
What a male animal does to the female when he penetrates her from the rear.

> THE DOG MOUNTED THE BITCH

N ―――――

Neck
To kiss for a long time.

> YOU SPENT MOST OF THE PARTY
> NECKING WITH THAT BLONDE

Nonce
Sexual offender.

Nubile
Physically very sexual and attractive – pronounced 'new-bile'.

> LOOK AT ALL THE NUBILE WOMEN
> ON THE BEACH

Nudger
Homosexual.

Nuptials
A formal, rather fancy, way of saying marriage or wedding.

Nympho
Short for nymphomaniac – very promiscuous young woman.

Nymphette
A sexually very attractive – but underage – girl.

 ―――――

Oldest profession
Prostitution.

One minute wonder
Man who has very quick orgasms.

One night stand:
A sexual relationship that only lasts one night.

> *SHE HAD A ONE NIGHT STAND WITH HIM*

On heat
Sexually excited. Usually said of female dogs when they are receptive to males but can also be applied to women who are in an aggressively sexual mood.

> *WHEN THE BITCH IS ON HEAT, EVERY DOG IN THE NEIGHBOURHOOD COMES SNIFFING AROUND*

Open minded
Tolerant about sexual variations and other differences between people.

> JOHN IS VERY OPEN MINDED. IN FACT, HE THINKS IT'S GOOD TO HAVE AN OPEN RELATIONSHIP

Open relationship
A relationship in which either partner is free to have affairs outside the relationship.

Orgy
A party where everyone has sex with each other – the adjective is orgiastic. Pronounced: 'or-jee'.

Out
'To out oneself' or 'to be outed' means to reveal publicly that a person is homosexual.

> HE OUTED HIMSELF BEFORE ANYONE ELSE COULD DO IT

P ———

Partner
One's steady life companion to whom one is not married.

Peach
An attractive girl – adjective is 'peachy'.

> SHE'S QUITE A PEACH

> SHE'S REALLY PEACHY

Peck
Quick kiss.

SHE GAVE ME A PECK ON MY CHEEK

Peeping Tom
See Voyeur.

Peep show
(also peek show) a live sex show.

Perve
A verb 'to perve'. This means to look at younger women with a sexual interest. Usually something that middle-aged men might do.

Pervert
This is an insulting word for someone who likes strange sexual acts.

PEOPLE WHO ARE INVOLVED IN
CHILD PORN ARE ALL PERVERTS

Pet
To engage in sexual foreplay. It becomes 'heavy petting' as it gets close to full sex.

THEY DID SOME HEAVY PETTING
IN THE BACK OF THE CAR

Peter
Penis – a peter beater is a masturbator.

Peter eater
Someone who likes oral sex.

Phoar!
The sound a man makes to signal that he has seen something sexy.

PHOAR! LOOK AT HER!

Pick up

As a noun this refers to a casual sex partner, the verb 'to pick up' is to meet and go out with someone of the opposite sex in the hope of some casual sex. A 'pick up joint' is a place single people go to meet other people.

> HE WENT WITH HIS PICK UP
> TO A CHEAP HOTEL

> IT'S EASY TO PICK UP GIRLS IN
> THE SHOPPING MALL

> THAT BAR IS A GOOD
> PICK UP JOINT

Pill

'The pill' always refers to the contraceptive pill for women.

> I'M ON THE PILL

Pimp

Someone who lives off the earnings of prostitutes. 'to pimp' is to market prostitutes.

> HE'S NO BETTER THAN A PIMP

> HE WOULD PIMP HIS OWN SISTER
> IF HE COULD

Play away from home

This is a football term which also means to have an affair.

Play / bat for the other side

Euphemism for being homosexual.

> HE'S NOT INTERESTED IN GIRLS. HE
> PLAYS FOR THE OTHER SIDE

Play hard to get
A game some women play when a man is attracted to them. They pretend not to be interested in order to stimulate the man to greater efforts.

Pocket billiards
'To play pocket billiards' is to put one's hands in one's pockets to touch one's own penis and testicles.

> STOP PLAYING POCKET BILLIARDS!

Pocket rocket
Penis.

Ponce
Another word for 'pimp'.

Ponce about
To act in a silly and unmanly way.

> HE STARTED TO PONCE ABOUT THE SHOP
> AND I GOT REALLY EMBARRASSED

Ponce off (someone)
To live off a prostitute's earnings – also used to describe someone who is always asking friends to provide spending money.

> GO AND PONCE OFF SOMEONE ELSE!

Popsie/popsy
Young attractive woman. Slightly old fashioned.

Prick-teaser
Woman who gets a man sexually excited but refuses to have sex.

Prime the pump
To play with the genitals as part of foreplay.

Promiscuous
Have sex with a lot of people.

> SHE'S HAD A FEW BOYFRIENDS BUT
> SHE'S NOT AT ALL PROMISCUOUS

Proposition
As a verb this means to make a clear sexual invitation.
American. Slightly dated.

> HE PROPOSITIONED HER

Provocative
Something that provokes a response – often a sexual
response.

> IN THE PHOTOGRAPH SHE WAS POSED
> VERY PROVOCATIVELY LYING AT THE EDGE
> OF THE SEA

Prozzie
Prostitute.

Pubes
Pubic hair – and, by extension, female genitals.

Pull (a woman)
To pick up a woman for sexual purposes.

> JOHN IS VERY GOOD AT PULLING WOMEN.
> I DON'T KNOW HOW HE DOES IT

Pussy whipped
Said of a man who is dominated by his wife or girlfriend.

Put it about
To have an active and varied sex life.

> HE HAS A REPUTATION FOR
> PUTTING IT ABOUT BUT I DON'T KNOW
> HOW TRUE THAT IS

Put out
Said of a woman who is sexually available.

> THEY SAY SHE PUTS OUT

Put the moves on
To start the process of seduction.

> HE PUT THE MOVES ON HER BUT
> SHE WASN'T INTERESTED

Queen
Older homosexual who acts in an over dramatic or effeminate way.

> I LIKE HIM BUT HE CAN BE A BIT
> OF AN OLD QUEEN SOMETIMES

Quickie
A fast act of sexual intercourse.

> WE'VE JUST GOT TIME FOR A QUICKIE

R

Randy:
Feeling in need of sex.

> GOD I'M FEELING SO RANDY

Raunchy
Full of sexually aggressive suggestiveness. (showing approval).

> SHE DANCED IN A RAUNCHY WAY WITH ALL THE GUYS

Red blooded
Normal, sexually active – usually restricted to heterosexual males.

Red-light district
Nightclub area of a town or city.

Ride
'A ride' is a woman assumed to be available for sexual purposes, 'to ride' is to have sex. Insulting.

> PEOPLE SAY SHE'S A GOOD RIDE

Rim
To stimulate the anus with lips or tongue.

Risqué
Euphemism meaning sexually explicit.

> HIS JOKES WERE A BIT RISQUÉ – BUT VERY FUNNY

Romp
To have a fun sexual experience.

> WE HAD A ROMP IN BED. IT WAS FUN

Rough trade
A homosexual term for a working-class sexual partner who is potentially violent.

> FROM TIME TO TIME, HE HAS A LIKING FOR A BIT OF ROUGH TRADE

Roundhead
A circumcised penis.

Roving eye
Said of a married man who likes to look at other women – and is used as a euphemism for married men who are known to have had a few affairs.

Run a train on
'To run a train on someone' is to force them to submit to having multiple sexual partners over a short period of time (see gang rape).

> ONE WAY OF FORCING A GIRL INTO PROSTITUTION IS TO PICK HER UP, TAKE HER TO AN APARTMENT AND RUN A TRAIN ON HER

S&M
Sado-masochism: 'sadism' means enjoying causing pain to others (from the French writer Marquis de Sade); 'masochism' is the enjoyment of pain that other people inflict on oneself (named after another writer, Leopold von Sacher-Masoch.). Pronounced: 'ess-and-em'.

Safe sex
Sex using a condom – or avoiding penetration.

Sandwich
Two people of one sex having sex with a person of the other sex.

Sappho
A lesbian – the adjective is 'sapphic' – named after an ancient Greek poetess.

Saucy
Sexually flirtatious, or rude in a jokey way.

DON'T BE SAUCY WITH ME

WHO WAS THAT SAUCY GIRL YOU WERE CHATTING TO?

Score
To achieve sex.

JOHN MET A COUPLE OF GIRLS LAST NIGHT AND HE MANAGED TO SCORE WITH ONE OF THEM

Seduce
To lead someone into having sex.

> SHE WENT TO HIS FLAT AND HE
> SEDUCED HER

Seducer/seductress
Man/woman who seduces.

Seductive
Sexually attractive and tempting.

> IT'S A SEDUCTIVE THOUGHT

> HE HAS A VERY SEDUCTIVE MANNER

Seven year itch
Supposedly, a man starts to get interested in other women seven years after getting married.

Sex act
Another way of saying sexual intercourse.

Sex appeal
To have sex appeal is to look sexy.

> HE'S GOT A LOT OF SEX APPEAL.

Sex bomb
Very attractive man or, more usually, woman.

> SOPHIA LOREN WAS A REAL SEX BOMB
> WHEN SHE WAS YOUNG

Sex drive
The physical energy that desires sex.

> WHAT'S WRONG WITH ME? I'VE GOT A
> VERY LOW SEX DRIVE

> HE'S GOT A VERY STRONG SEX DRIVE.
> HE HAS TO DO IT TWO OR THREE TIMES
> EVERY DAY

Sexism
Discrimination against a person on grounds of sex. A person
who does this is a sexist.

Sexed up
To be sexually excited.

> I GOT HER ALL SEXED UP AND WE
> HAD A LOT OF FUN

Sex kitten
Young woman with a lot of sex appeal.

> BRIGIT BARDOT WAS THE
> CLASSIC SEX KITTEN

Sex machine
A man who is very virile.

Sexploits
Cheap newspaper word for sexual activities (sex + exploits).

Sex starved
The feeling of frustration at not getting enough sex.

> THE SEX STARVED SAILORS KEPT THE TOWN
> BROTHELS BUSY FOR A WHOLE WEEK

Sex symbol
A person, male or female, usually a film star, who represents a physical ideal.

Sexual abuse
Any coerced sexual contact from touching to rape – usually of children.

SHE WAS SEXUALLY ABUSED BY ONE OF HER UNCLES WHEN SHE WAS A YOUNG GIRL

Sexual assault
Any unwanted sexual contact – but not including rape.

Sexual harassment
Unwanted sexual attention. Harassment usually has the idea of repetitive action but nowadays even a single act of sex-related annoyance can be considered harassment.

Sexual innuendo
Statements that can have a hidden sexual meaning.

Shack up with

To live together even though not married – usually temporarily. Other words with same meaning are: 'to live with someone' and 'to cohabit with someone' (formal).

> AT THE MOMENT SHE'S SHACKING UP WITH TED – BUT I DON'T THINK IT'S A PERMANENT ARRANGEMENT

Shameless

A disapproving word said of a woman who is happy to express her interest in sex or who dresses in an openly sexual way.

> SHE IS A SHAMELESS HUSSY!

Shemale

Transvestite or transsexual.

Shenanigans

Naughty games, messing about, trickery and cheating.

> I GOT TIRED OF HIS SEXUAL SHENANIGANS AND SO I DIVORCED HIM

Short and curlies

The phrase is 'to have someone by the short and curlies'. The 'short and curlies' are the pubic hairs. This expression means to have someone in one's complete control (unwillingly).

> I CAN'T DO ANYTHING TO STOP YOU. YOU'VE GOT ME BY THE SHORT AND CURLIES

Short time

A quick session with a prostitute.

Siren
A beautiful woman who is also dangerous and should therefore be avoided.

Six pack
Means either
i) six cans of beer
ii) well defined stomach muscles.

> HE WORKS OUT IN THE GYM EVERYDAY. HE'S GOT A GREAT SIX PACK

Skirt chaser
Man who chases after women.

Sleaze
Anything distasteful and disgusting – often used in relation to pornography.

> FROM TIME TO TIME I ENJOY A LITTLE SLEAZE

Sleazebag
Distasteful person.

Sleaze monger
Person who sells pornography.

Sleazy
Unpleasant and distasteful.

> IT'S A REALLY SLEAZY CLUB. YOU WOULDN'T LIKE IT

Sloppy seconds
What a second man is offered immediately after a first man
has had sex with a woman.

> MARY SCREWED JOHN FIRST AND
> THEN I HAD SLOPPY SECONDS

Slut puppy
a) a lesbian or
b) a promiscuous woman.

Smack
Quick kiss on the cheeks.

> SHE GAVE ME A SMACK ON BOTH CHEEKS

Smitten
'To be smitten by someone' is to have fallen in love with
someone.

> SHE'S COMPLETELY SMITTEN

Smooch
To kiss and caress – often while standing or dancing.

> WE SMOOCHED TO AN OLD FRANK
> SINATRA SONG

Smut
Another word for pornography. The adjective is 'smutty' –
meaning dirty in a sexual way.

> HIS UNCLE LIKES TO TELL SMUTTY JOKES.
> IT'S A BIT EMBARRASSING

Snip
'To have the snip' means to have a vasectomy.

> I'VE HAD THE SNIP SO I CAN'T HAVE
> ANY MORE CHILDREN

Snog
Long, passionate kiss.

Softcore porn
Pictures of naked men or women in sensual poses – but not having sex.

Soul kiss
Deep kiss with tongue play (also: French kiss).

Sow wild oats
This is said of a young man who has an active sex life.

> HE DOESN'T WANT TO SETTLE DOWN
> JUST YET. HE'S HAVING TOO MUCH FUN
> SOWING WILD OATS

Squeeze
Dismissive term for female companion.

> JOHN WENT TO THE PARTY WITH
> HIS LATEST SQUEEZE

Stag party
Male only party for groom – usually the night before the wedding.

Stallion
Sexually strong male.

Stand someone up
To not turn up for a date.

> WE ARRANGED TO MEET AT 8PM
> BUT SHE STOOD ME UP!

Starkers
Naked.

> SHE RAN ACROSS THE FOOTBALL FIELD
> COMPLETELY STARKERS

STDs
Acronym for Sexually Transmitted Diseases.

Straight
Means 'normal heterosexual person' – can also be used as an adjective to mean 'normal' or 'honest'. If a criminal 'goes straight' – it means he has left behind his life of crime.

> HE'S NOT GAY. HE'S STRAIGHT

> HE ONLY LIKES STRAIGHT SEX. HE
> DOESN'T GO FOR ANYTHING KINKY

Streaker
Person who runs naked in a very public place i.e. during a football match.

Strumpet
Prostitute (old fashioned).

Stud
Sexually strong male.

Sugar daddy
Wealthy older man who provides money and presents for young mistress.

Sultry
Sexy, hot, suggesting inner passions that need to be released.

> **SHE GAVE ME A LONG SULTRY LOOK AND I WENT WEAK AT THE KNEES**

Swing
A verb meaning: to exchange husbands and wives, or have an affair, or to enjoy an active and varied sex life.

> **DO YOU LIKE TO SWING?**

Swinger
Person who swings.

Swing party
Orgy.

T ————

Talent
Attractive girl(s).

> **THERE WASN'T MUCH TALENT AT THE PARTY**

Talk dirty
Say bad words (often while being affectionate).

> **I DON'T LIKE PEOPLE WHO TALK DIRTY**

> **I LIKE A WOMAN WHO TALKS DIRTY WHILE WE'RE MAKING LOVE**

Tart
Sexually available. Cheap, low-class woman.

Tiger/Tigress
Someone who is extremely enthusiastic in bed.

Toy boy
Young male lover of older woman.

Threesome
Sex involving three people (also: foursome etc.).

Thrills
Things that sexually excite you.

> **HE GETS HIS THRILLS FROM BEING SPANKED**

Titfuck
The stimulation of the penis between a woman's breasts.

Titillate
Noun titillation: to stimulate sexually.

> **IT'S SUPPOSED TO BE PORN BUT I
> DIDN'T FIND IT VERY TITILLATING**

Touch up
To touch (someone's) genitals to get him or her sexually excited.

Town bike
A local town prostitute or a girl who everyone has 'ridden'.

Tranny
Abbreviation of transvestite (man who wears women's clothes) or transsexual. (someone who has had a sex change operation).

Triangle
A continuing – but problematic – sexual relationship in which one person is carrying on two affairs at the same time.

Trick
A prostitute's word for a customer or the act of having sex with a customer.

IT'S A SLOW NIGHT. I HAVEN'T TURNED A SINGLE TRICK YET

Troilism
Formal word for three in a bed having sex.

Tubes, to tie
A woman who has her tubes tied has had an operation to prevent eggs from her ovaries being able to come down the fallopian tube where they might be fertilized by semen – a form of permanent birth control.

> *SHE'S GOING TO HAVE HER TUBES TIED*

Turn on
To excite sexually (also noun: a turn on) – can also mean to introduce someone to something enjoyable. The opposite is turn off.

> *THE WAY HE LOOKED AT ME WAS A REAL TURN ON*

> *I TURNED HIM ON TO CUBAN MUSIC*

> *WE DANCED AND SMOOCHED FOR HOURS. I GOT REALLY TURNED ON*

> *BAD BREATH IS A REAL TURN OFF*

Tussle
'To have a tussle between the sheets' is to have sex.

Two-time
'To two-time someone' is to cheat or deceive someone. More specifically it means to have other lovers. Noun form: a two-timer, adjective: two-timing.

> *HE'S A TWO-TIMING BASTARD*

> *I'VE JUST DISCOVERED SHE HAS BEEN TWO-TIMING ME*

U,V ———

Undies
Abbreviation for underpants.

Unfaithful
If someone is unfaithful they are having sex outside their main relationship.

> **I'VE NEVER BEEN UNFAITHFUL TO MY WIFE**

Up for it
Eager and enthusiastic – especially something that is a little naughty or risky.

> **I'M UP FOR SOME HANKY PANKY IF YOU ARE**

> **SHE WANTS THE TV COMPANY TO KNOW THAT SHE'S AN UP-FOR-IT KIND OF GIRL**

Vamp
A disapproving word to describe an attractive woman who uses her beauty to get what she wants from a man. The idea is that she bleeds him dry. (old fashioned). More modern is to call a woman a vampire.

Vanilla sex
Bland sex – sex that is straight and unexciting.

VD
This is an abbreviation for Venereal Disease ie any of the diseases connected with sex. A bit old fashioned – generally referred to now as STDs (Sexually Transmitted Diseases).

Vibrator
A vibrating dildo.

Vice
This is the legal word that refers to immoral acts and the sex industry. The police section in charge of arresting prostitutes is known as the vice squad.

Vice girl
Newspaper language for prostitute or call girl.

Virile
Sexually strong.

> **BALD MEN ARE SUPPOSEDLY MORE VIRILE THAN MEN WITH LOTS OF HAIR**

Virtual sex
Sexual activity mediated by computer – not real sex.

Voyeur
A man who gets sexual thrills from secretly watching people having sex or getting undressed. (also: peeping tom).

W,X,Y,Z ———

Wanton
Sexually loose – usually applied to women (slightly old fashioned).

> **I FIND HER WANTON BEHAVIOUR QUITE DISGUSTING!**

Water sports
In a sexual context these refer to urination as part of sex play.

Well endowed
Said of a woman who has large breasts.

Well hung
Said of a male who has a large penis.

Wet dream
A sexy dream that causes a man to have an orgasm in his sleep.

Wet one's pants
(Of a woman) to get sexually excited.

> I REALLY FANCY HIM. EVERY TIME I SEE HIM I WET MY PANTS

Wham bam, thank you ma'am
Male reference to a quickly completed sex act.

> I HAD A QUICK WHAM BAM THANK YOU MA'AM AND THEN IT WAS BACK TO WORK

Whisper sweet nothings
This means to whisper soft words of love in the ear of the beloved.

> HE WHISPERED SWEET NOTHINGS INTO HER EAR

Wiggle
To move one's hips in a sexually alluring way.

> HEY GIRL! WIGGLE THOSE HIPS!

Wolf
A man who wishes to take sexual advantage of women.

> **BE CAREFUL OF HIM. HE HAS A REPUTATION FOR BEING A WOLF**

Wolf whistle
The special whistle that a man makes when he sees an attractive woman and wishes to let her know.

Womaniser
A man who is constantly in the company of different women.

Woman of pleasure
A prostitute.

You-know-what
A way of referring to genitals.

> **SHE TOOK OFF ALL HER CLOTHES AND STARTED TO SHAKE HER YOU-KNOW-WHAT RIGHT IN FRONT OF MY FACE**

X-rated:
Pornographic, for adults only – based on an old way of classifying films.

> **IT'S AN X RATED FILM**

Ways of saying:
She's beautiful! He's handsome!

Nice

Nouns:
(For women) a stunner, a knock out.
(For men) a hunk.

Adjectives:
Good looking, stunning, striking, dishy, cute,
drop-dead gorgeous, fanciable, sexy, mouth watering.

Verbs:
Turns (one) on.

US English:

Slightly vulgar
Babe, eye candy, foxy chick.

More vulgar:
Piece of ass, piece of tail, hottie.

British English:

Slightly vulgar
Crumpet, cracker, corker, bit of all right, looker, hot stuff,
cutie.

More Vulgar
Bit of arse, bit of fluff, tottie, nookie, piece of skirt.

SHE'S A BIT OF A LOOKER

SHE'S A KNOCK OUT

SHE'S A BIT OF ALL RIGHT

SHE'S A REAL CUTIE

HE'S QUITE DISHY, DON'T YOU THINK?

HE WAS DROP DEAD GORGEOUS

HE'S QUITE STRIKING I SUPPOSE
BUT HE DOESN'T TURN ME ON

HE'S REALLY VERY FANCIABLE

It is an interesting fact that Americans tend to use different words than British speakers when they are being most vulgar but the nice words tend to be used equally in both countries. It should be noted that women, generally speaking, will consider the more vulgar words – which can only refer to females – to be offensive. The nice words are used by both men and women to refer to each other.

Ways of suggesting that women are sexually available

Men are always hopeful that an attractive woman will be sexually available. Here are some of the things they might say:

Less Vulgar
Tart, sexpot, goer

More Vulgar
Easy ride, easy lay, easy meat, floozy, hot to trot

Birth control

Of course, when a woman makes love with a man she needs to make sure she doesn't get pregnant. The most common form of protection, recommended as a form of safe sex is the condom.

Key words

A durex*	A rubber	A johnny
A cock sock	A raincoat	A French letter
A prophylactic	protection	A protective

named after the company that makes them.

> I'LL GO ALL THE WAY IF YOU USE A RUBBER

> PUT ON THE COCK SOCK AND LET'S DO IT

> HE BOUGHT A PACKET OF PROTECTIVES JUST IN CASE

Forms of protection that a woman can take

To be on the pill: *to use a contraceptive pill*

To use a Dutch cap: *to insert a barrier covered with spermicidal cream*

To have a coil: *to have a small twisted piece of plastic placed in the uterus*

> SHE DOESN'T LIKE BEING ON THE PILL

> SHE PREFERS TO USE A DUTCH CAP

If birth control isn't used we can say:

> THEY LIKE TO HAVE SEX SKIN TO SKIN

> THEY LIKE RIDING BAREBACK

> I ALWAYS INSIST ON SAFE SEX

Pregnancy

But if the woman is not on the pill and the man doesn't use protection, then the result of a love making session might be that she will get pregnant. Here are some vulgar expressions for that state.

Key words:

> ### Nice word:
> *Expecting.*
>
> ---
>
> ### Vulgar phrases
> *Get (someone) into trouble, be knocked up, have a bun in the oven, join the pudding club, be preggers, be prego, be up the pole (duff/kite), be in the family way.*

SHE'S EXPECTING

SHE'S GOT KNOCKED UP

HE GOT HER INTO TROUBLE

SHE'S GOT A BUN IN THE OVEN

SHE'S JOINED THE PUDDING CLUB

SHE'S PREGO

SHE'S PREGGERS

SHE'S UP THE DUFF!

SHE'S UP THE POLE

SHE'S IN THE FAMILY WAY

Sexually transmitted diseases

Safe sex is advisable to avoid catching an 'STD' – a sexually transmitted disease, The most common diseases are syphilis and gonorrhoea - but the most devastating is AIDS. AIDS is so devastating a disease that up till now no-one has come up with a vulgar euphemism for it but the other two diseases are commonly known as 'the clap' and 'the pox'.

> HE'S CAUGHT A DOSE OF THE CLAP

> HE'S GOT A DOSE OF THE POX

Associated expressions

Poxy

This is an adjective meaning disgusting or contemptible.

> SHE'S A POXY BITCH

> YOU POXY SON OF A BITCH!

Clapped out

This means worn out, no longer useful. Usually used of cars or other machines, it can also be used of people.

> IT'S A CLAPPED OUT CITROEN

> SHE'S A CLAPPED OUT OLD WHORE

TART

To tart oneself up
This is a phrase used by women meaning to make a special effort to look attractive.

> I'M GOING TO TART MYSELF UP FOR THE PARTY

> SHOULD WE TART OURSELVES UP OR SHOULD WE GO DRESSED AS WE ARE?

To tart something up
To redecorate a place – usually in a cheap and vulgar way.

> IT WAS A NICE RESTAURANT UNTIL THEY TARTED IT UP

To be tarted up
To have been redecorated – usually not in a good way.

> THE RESTAURANT HAS BEEN ALL TARTED UP. IT REALLY LOOKS AWFUL

Tarty
This is an adjective meaning to do something in a cheap and vulgar way – i.e. like a prostitute.

> SHE LIKES TO DRESS UP IN A REALLY TARTY WAY

The Sex Industry

1: Prostitutes

Prostitution is often referred to as 'the oldest profession'.

Women

In the old days a prostitute might be called 'a lady of easy virtue', 'a harlot' or a 'street walker' nowadays she is more likely to be referred to by one of the following terms:

Low class:
An alley cat, a bar girl, a floozy, a dolly, a doxy, a cruiser, a hooker, a hustler, a nighthawk, a working girl, a goodtime girl.

Higher class
A business girl, a call girl, an escort.

Female prostitutes are often controlled by a man:
A pimp, a pander, an ass peddler, a stable boss.

Men

There are of course male prostitutes as well. The standard term for a man who is paid to be a companion to a woman is 'gigolo'.

Words for homosexual male prostitutes
A chicken, a rent boy, a bunny, a call boy, a punk, a midnight cowboy

Associated words

All nighter: *all night session*
Short time: *a session lasting one completed sex act*
A freebie: *a free anything, it also refers to a prostitute giving sex for free.*
On the game: *working as a prostitute*

2: Brothels

Brothels are places where you can go to have paid sex with someone. Such places have existed throughout history and their popularity can be seen from the wide number of expressions used to refer to them.

A bawdy house,	**A bordello,**
A cat house,	**A chicken ranch,**
A chippie joint,	**A fancy house,**
Fleshpot,	**Flesh market,**
House of ill repute	**A massage parlour,**
A dive*	

*a dive is really a low class bar or nightclub where you are likely to meet 'a working girl'.

*The person in charge of a brothel is often a woman known as **the madam, the bawd, the hostess** or the **mother superior**. She will be helped by a bouncer – a man whose job is to get rid of customers who are causing a disturbance*

"THE ZIPLESS FUCK IS ABSOLUTELY PURE. IT IS FREE OF ULTERIOR MOTIVES. THERE IS NO POWER GAME. THE MAN IS NOT 'TAKING' AND THE WOMAN IS NOT 'GIVING'... THE ZIPLESS FUCK IS THE PUREST THING THERE IS. AND IT IS RARER THAN THE UNICORN."

Erica Jong

3: Entertainment

Most cities have a red light district – an area where there are bars, nightclubs and prostitutes and other forms of 'adult entertainment'.

The Strip Club: *a club where there are strippers*

Stripper: *girl whose job is to take off her clothes suggestively*

Striptease: *the act of taking off clothes in a slow and suggestive manner*

Bump and grind: *move the hips in a simulation of sex*

G-string/thong: *a very small piece of cloth covering the dancer's genitals*

Leg show: *striptease that stops before total nudity*

Exotic dancer: *dancers who perform sexually suggestive dances: also known as **lap dancers, pole dancers, table dancers***

Bars

Girlie bar: *bars where there are a lot of girls, 'hostesses' who will keep a man company for the price of a drink*

Topless bar: *bar where the girls don't wear tops*

Hostess bar: *a high class girlie bar (also known as an escort bar)*

Go-Go bar: *a bar where there are go-go dancers – i.e. dancers wearing bikinis at most – who dance on a raised stage in the middle of the bar*

Bar fine: *fee you pay to take a girl out of a bar*

4: Pornography

Here is some vocabulary associated with pornography

Porn: *pornographic material*

Porno: *relating to pornography*

Porn films: *pornographic films: Also known as* **blue movies, skin flicks** *or* **stag films**

Porn mag: *pornographic magazines*

Porn shop: *a place selling pornographic material*

Peep show: *a coin machine that shows short sections of films. Also refers to exhibitions of live sexual performances*

Pornographic Sex Acts

Facial: *a man ejaculating on to the face of his partner*

Sandwich: *sex with two members of the opposite sex – more specifically simultaneous vaginal and anal sex with one woman and two men*

Finger/Fist fuck: *a man (or woman) places a finger/fist into the vagina of a woman*

Tit fuck: *a man places his penis between a woman's breasts*

Cumshot: *photographic image of ejaculation. Also known as the money shot*

Continued on next page...

4: Pornography

Some associated words

Porn magazines: *these are known as* **porn mags** *or* **skin mags** *or* **wank mags**. *A magazine showing naked men is a* **fag mag**

Softcore: *pictures of nudity but no sex acts*

Hardcore: *pictures of sex acts*

Pinup: *picture of an attractive naked woman (usually)*

Pinup girl: *a model who specialises in posing for pinup pictures.*

Centrefold: *the glossy photograph in the centre of a magazine like Playboy*

Cover girl: *a female model who appears on front covers of magazines*

Page 3 girl: *a model who poses for softcore nude shots published by The Sun – a British newspaper*

Cheesecake: *erotic pictures of women, also the models who pose for these pictures*

Beefcake: *erotic pictures of men, also the male models who pose for them.*

Sex scenes are often described as:

Hot	*Steamy*
Sizzling	*Mouth watering*
Juicy	*Explicit*

INDEX ———

A

B

The
Essential
Guide

*to the curses,
swear words,
obscenities, insults,
profanities and
sex slang of
contemporary English*

This book cannot be bought in a bookshop.
It is only available from

www.vulgarenglish.com

Buy your own copy today!!!

NOTES ────────

Make notes on the following pages of any
additional interesting words or phrases you hear...

Notes

Notes

Notes

Notes

Notes

Notes

Notes

Notes